The Back Stage Book of New American Short Plays

The Back Stage Book of

NEW AMERICAN SHORT PLAYS

20 Plays

20 Fresh New Voices

EDITED BY CRAIG LUCAS

BACK STAGE BOOKS/New York

to Bartlett Sher and everyone at the
Intiman Theater

Senior Editor: Mark Glubke

Project Editor: Ross Plotkin

Cover Design: Donna Rafery, Apptex International Corp.

Interior Design: Leah Lococo

Production Manager: Hector Campbell

First published in 2004 by Back Stage Books,

an imprint of Watson-Guptill Publications,

a division of VNU Business Media, Inc.,

770 Broadway, New York, NY 10003

www.wgpub.com.com

Library of Congress Control Number: 2004108941

ISBN: 0-8230-8801-1 (Hardcover)

ISBN: 0-8230-8804-9 (Paperback)

Manufactured in the United States of America

First printing 2004

1 2 3 4 5 6 7 8 9 / 11 10 09 08 07 06 05 04

Table of Contents

INTRODUCTION

There's been an animated, verging-on-raucous debate in my home from the moment the plays submitted for this anthology began to arrive in bundles like the early-morning edition.

One faction herein feels that it's pointless to attempt to relate why one prefers a certain play over another. "At the very least you should tell the nice people to *read* the plays before they are dragged through your dreary introduction." They feel that good plays speak best for themselves, and that, in Kurt Vonnegut's words, "It is criminal to explain works of art."

Another bloc holds that it is useful to articulate the standards one employs; these things should not be entirely instinctual or one risks becoming smug or lazy, even prejudicial in ways that are at best unconscious: "I know what I like and goddamit I don't care if it's . . ." Fill in blank.

A third segment, a minority of one, maintains there are no unchanging rules for making or appreciating art, and new work typically meets all kinds of resistance; therefore, it is often valuable for champions of the new to articulate the virtues they perceive in the work. I agree with her. (The hoary ghost of W.H. Auden, slumped in the corner with the wet stump of a Gauloise staining his stubby fingers, intones: "In the prison of his days, teach the free man how to praise." Oyez, oyez.) A sudden convert to this cause then cautions, "Okay, but if you're going to break the rules, you'd better be pretty damn brilliant."

"That may all be so," an unidentified voice from the floor pipes in, "But when a received wisdom outlives its usefulness, it is painfully clear to one and all; things that were once funny as satire, say, such as the banality of TV coverage of the entertainment industry, are no longer that—why waste the print to point out what everyone can see?"

Yet another . . . wait a minute, how many people do I live with, anyway? Well, it so happens I'm on my own this week. Which is how things have gotten so rowdy. It's a kind of unscripted play here, led by a colorful if churlish assortment of Gestalt figureheads, a not-at-all uncommon colloquy of conflicting proponents, naysayers, idealists, pundits, and other undesirables, filled with yearnings and dire warnings. These include the Conservative Critic (Dad), the Socialist Pioneer (Brecht and his courageous disciples; only a portion are here, the other half are at a MoveOn meeting), the Genius to Whom No Obvious Rules Apply (Beckett and the Beckett-manques, *you know who you are*), the Shamefully Indifferent Philistine who likes musicals and doesn't worry about much else (the eight-year-old still alive in some of us, that lonely little girl who self-identifies as a boy and is still trying to get her hands on an illegal recording of the final performance of *Flahooley!*), the Patient Teacher/Visionary, the Hotheaded Firebrand who has a real problem with authority, etc.

In order to quiet things down, I have appointed myself secretary, assembling the basic arguments as they center around the plays we have chosen. Needless to say, I don't always agree with everything said, and in a few years I expect to be shocked to see what some of these clowns believed. But here we go: "What Makes a Good One-Act Play," written by the Official Selection Committee:

First and foremost, plays should be entertaining. "But what does that mean?" Settle down; already we're in contention. The Adolescent *enlightens* us, "If my Dad were editing this anthology, he would have steered clear of all the plays that made him feel sad or uncomfortable or made him think too much." Well, Dad is actually at the table, as suggested earlier, and we have learned through experience to hear him out and then be sure to consult with others. It's all a matter of dialectics, then, this defining of 'entertainment'—no fixed meter to cling to. "Some are entertained by dross!" "Yeah, and some by pretentious high-flown fake-intellectual blather, too." Gavel sounds. Diminishing murmurs.

Truthfully, Dad is quite useful to have around, because a lot of the other folks renting out skullspace have a strong preference for challenging work, for connecting the dots themselves; they bristle at being told what to think or feel, and they can be belligerent about it. They chose

Neena Beber's gorgeous *A Body of Water* wherein a young couple at the beach discusses whether or not one of them is too fat between revelations of what will befall both of them in the full breadth of time. Well, it's either that, or the same two look back at their day at the beach from the long perspective of old age. Actually, it might be both. And Joseph Goodrich's *White Russian*, an elegy for three émigrés caught up in a terrible and modern—I think it's modern—civil war; they speak a cultured patois in the face of unimaginable slaughter and brutality; but why one of them should take the rash and completely shocking action they do at the end of the tale is left for us to grapple with. Another kind of difficulty, if you will, surfaces in Jeff Tabnick's finely-tuned slice of lowlife, *Dissatisfaction #4*. The couple speaking are not, in fact, talking about what they are talking about. They're talking about something they don't really ever "talk about," quite. Tabnick's ear for spoken American speech of a certain lilt and skew is so spot-on, not a few of us are filled with envy, and we look forward to more. '*Hear hear*'s.

The largest resident constituency wants a play, assuming it has already been deemed entertaining by a sufficient number of taste-mongers, to be *theatrical*—to use language inventively, to juggle and flash metaphors, to create imagery that is not wholly reliant on cameras and computers, certainly *never* on projections, to give virtuoso actors a chance to steal our breath away, to surprise, give us the taste of real imagination, anything, really, that makes it worth leaving your house and paying good money and putting up with people who are sneezing on you and jingling their titanium bracelets as they lean forward to explain things out loud to their nonegenarian uncles whose headsets are setting their hearing aids off into marvelous squeals of spine-tingling disarray. Otherwise, why not stay home and watch TV? Now that there's HBO and Blockbuster, theater has to work much harder. These folks are big proponents of Christopher Shinn's elegant *The Sleepers*, which employs a theatrical device neatly enabling us to see, and yet not be distracted by, the sexual goings-on which are *not* the real event at the heart of the proceedings, but very much part of how we might

understand that which is. ("Please stop Miss Henry James," mutters
the Evil Theater Queen to my right.) David Schulner's *Hope (and
Charles)* gives us two completely different, but completely related, per-
spectives on a first date. No movie could do it such justice; TV would
turn it into a skit. Bathsheba Doran enables us, in *2 Soldiers*, to witness
a warrior from an ancient era encountering one from ours; it is heart-
breaking, and hilariously funny to boot. So moved.

Some of my fellow cranial-mates go to the theater to see their own
experience enlightened and mirrored back with poignancy or devastat-
ing wit or deep perceptiveness or all of the above. They are cheering
loudest for anton dudley's *Davy and Stu*, which conveys the awful
combo platter of tenderness, immature cruelty, lust, and loneliness that
can live inside a teenage love affair. Take a look at the first and last
lines of his play; this guy has a rare gift. As does Neena Beber (yes,
there are two of her plays included) who slices right into the artery
of altruism's beef with individual, self-imposed limits in *Help*; seldom
have liberal yearnings been more painfully exposed, or empathy and
cold-eyed clarity made to stand so nakedly side by side. Andrew
Dainoff's grand aria, *All We Can Handle*, tells an unbearably sad tale
of loss. It might come to seem excessive and unlikely to those who have
been fortunate enough to miss fate's brutally relentless clubbings ("*So
far*," adds Evil Theater Queen), but for those of us who have not, and
for whom loss is a most persistent houseguest, it speaks to our condition
like no other play. In Mary Gallagher's *Perfect*, the eternal struggle
between one's convictions and the greater good of our dating options
is efficiently nailed. Case closed. *Foul Territory* by Craig Wright also
takes on misfortune's unjust hand, this time hilariously and with full
equipoise and sanguinity. Many of us laughed out loud. "If a play does
no more than give people joy, it has aided mankind." Brecht. (His girls
are trimming his nose and ear hairs.)

Another contingent prefers to see through a clear window onto
other people's lives *unlike* their own. They most enjoy the chance to
widen the circle of Us with new members of what was only-moments-
before Them. Of course, this sort of rearranging all depends on where

you stand, and what circles have been drawn around you by some distracted messenger of those indifferent gods of ours—for those currently living in post-colonial squalor of almost any desperately poor African nation, *Salvage Baas* by Brian Silberman will provide neither news nor comfort. What it will offer is the palpable agony of powerlessness fighting off despair in the full-throated, elevated poetry of song. Jason Grote's *Kawaisoo (The Pity of Things)* does much the same for those to whom past and soon-to-be misfortunes spin one around in a Mixmaster of sheer ickiness, sorrow, and brightly-absurdist rage, and it does so with style and an eccentric wit.

Okay, there's one last crackpot at the table, and that's the Playwright. S/he likes one particular thing more than all others, and it's seeing the mess of life recreated, distilled, laid out like an exploded kitchen supply warehouse. This one feels that art's highest purpose is to join us in a reawakened sense of the outrageous beauty and horror of what it means to be alive—which is never neat; seldom nice; often bark-out-loud-like-a-trained-seal funny; full of stumblings and misspoken blurtings; humiliatingly failed attempts both noble and ig-; and all around, birth-to-death, everywhere-you-look, major mindfucks. Murphy's Law reigns. (Murphy's Law, which is frequently twisted out of shape by the forces of Dumbing Down, actually reads, in the words of Airforce Captain Murphy, "If there's more than one way to do a job and one of those ways will end in disaster, then somebody will do it that way.")

The Playwright doesn't much care for a lot of TV and movies (and theater, too, honestly) because the mess has been cleaned up. Everything is like clockwork. Bad farce. Drama of resolution. *Or* it's fake mess. When watching a story unfold, the Playwright wants to believe that things are being said and done for the very first time, executed always with the firm belief that one will now succeed, this time it's going to work, goddamit—this followed most often by that warm, runny egg slipping down your chin and coming to rest on the front of your silvery-sheer, incredibly expensive shirt right around your newly-pert nipples, suddenly visible from the moon.

The rest of the work here is particularly good at capturing this messy state of affairs. Scott Organ's two plays, *China* and *The Mulligan*, both end in graceful chagrin; both audience and protagonist have had the rug pulled out from under them, and in neither case did the folks at this table see it coming. In *Defusion*, Brooke Berman lovingly guides you to expect one kind of love story and then hands you a whole other ball of wax in the clinch. Victor Lodato's plainspoken and dry-eyed *Dear Sara Jane* is about the mess of waiting for someone fighting far away in a war impossible to imagine (as all wars surely are); she is now married to a creature who has experienced the worst of humanity and may well be coming home with this lethally viral knowledge.

Hippie Van Gumdrop by Dan LeFranc gives us two sisters rummaging through their dead mother's home which, in this case, is a rusty van; is there anything at all here worth saving? Anne Ziegler's *Sad Song* manages to provide a glimpse of late adolescence or early adulthood — whatever you call it, it's that appalling time when you don't have any idea what damage you are doing to other people, or yourself, as you blithely flail and stumble around trying to hammer together some sort of Self — a "personality," a set of likes and dislikes, a job, a mate, a *life*; the results are both tender and terribly bitter. Finally, Joan Ackermann, whose plays I have always loved, gives us a surprisingly generous resolution to one of life's most hideous experiences — an actor's audition — in *The Second Beam*.

Historically, societies have been assessed, along with many other indicators, by the accomplishments and aspirations of their artists. Fifth Century B.C. Greece and Elizabethan England gave Western civilization it's two greatest outcroppings of theatrical brilliance. So far. Though many Americans in this moment find themselves in a white heat over the policies and actions of their government and fellow citizenry, the voices and level of artistry evinced in these plays is a much-needed spot of hope in a landscape of greed, devastation, øand insupportable self-satisfaction.

Read.

CRAIG LUCAS, Seattle, July 2004

THE SECOND BEAM

A short play by
Joan Ackermann

CHARACTERS:

Georgia

Jennifer

Meg

Casting Agent

Patti Scharer

PLACE:

An audition waiting room.

JOAN ACKERMANN is co-founder and artistic director of Mixed Company Theatre in Great Barrington, Massachusetts, now in its twenty-third year. Her plays include *Zara Spook and Other Lures, Stanton's Garage, The Batting Cage, Don't Ride the Clutch, Bed and Breakfast, Rescuing Greenland, A Knight at the Theatre, My New York Hit, Back Story, Off the Map, Marcus is Walking,* and *Isabella: A Young Physician's Primer on the Perils of Love,* a musical for which she wrote the music and lyrics. She adapted *Off the Map* into a screenplay directed by Campbell Scott and starring Joan Allen and Sam Elliot. Her plays have been produced at The Vineyard Theatre, The Guthrie Theatre, Circle Rep, the George Street Theatre, Cleveland Playhouse, Shakespeare & Company, the Berkshire Theatre Festival, Mark Taper Forum, and the Atlantic Theatre Company.

The Second Beam was produced at Mixed Company in February 2004, directed by Michael Dowling.

In an audition waiting room, three women—GEORGIA, JENNIFER, *and* MEG—sit on folded chairs and study pages from a script. They are all dressed in lab coats as scientists. After a moment, a casting agent opens a door and sticks her head in.

CASTING AGENT: Georgia? [GEORGIA *smiles up at her, grabs her stuff and exits. The other two smile at her as she exits into the audition room, closing the door behind her.* MEG *is the older of the two, more mature, grounded.* JENNIFER *is soft-spoken, sweet.*]

JENNIFER: [*Approaching* MEG.] Pardon me . . . Do you have a tissue? [MEG *opens her bag and gives her one. Goes back to studying.* JENNIFER *sits down with the tissue and very discreetly wipes under both her armpits.*] You were at *The Flannerys.* [MEG *looks at her blankly.*] You read for the sister. Of the boxer, with the bad hand. The malpractice suit.

MEG: [*Remembering.*] Oh. Right.

JENNIFER: I heard that show didn't get picked up. You were at *Mind of a Married Man,* too. The jockey's wife. [*Concerned.*] Are you memorizing that?

MEG: [*Friendly.*] No. No, just studying. [*Pause.*]

JENNIFER: Do you happen to know who got the part?

MEG: Which part. The sister, of the boxer?

JENNIFER: No. Yes.

MEG: Or the jockey's wife.

JENNIFER: Either. Both.

MEG: Well, the same actress got them both.

JENNIFER: Patti Scharer?

MEG: Patti Scharer.

JENNIFER: I knew it. Patti Scharer. Patti Scharer. Every part my agent sends me out on, every single part it seems, Patti Scharer gets. Care for a mint? [MEG *shakes her head no, takes out a lipstick and puts some on, looking at herself in a small compact mirror.*] Are you doing an accent?

MEG: Accent?

JENNIFER: For the scientist.

MEG: What kind of accent?

JENNIFER: Foreign.

MEG: I think she's American. [*Pause.*]

JENNIFER: [*Concerned.*] So you're not doing an accent? [MEG *shakes her head, goes back to studying the pages.*] I was going to do a French accent. Madame Curie. The scientist. You don't think I should?

MEG: If you've worked on it that way. It's a choice.

JENNIFER: Yes, it is. It's a choice. [*Pause.*] I never know about choices. My agent always says they like it when you make a choice, but I'm not so sure. I've been making choices, strong choices, but . . . they haven't really been panning out for me. [*She discreetly picks something out from between her teeth.*] I really need the work. I really, really, really need the work. I'm sorry, I'll let you concentrate. [*Pause.*] Have you read for him before? [MEG *looks at her.*] Ethan Schroeder. The director. Have you read for him? [MEG *nods. Goes back to her pages, concentrat-*

ing.] My friend Annette says he's a monster. She read for him for a movie of the week and he ate his lunch the entire time.

MEG: He can be a jerk.

JENNIFER: That's all I need. [*She sighs, smooths her skirt.*] Can I just ask you . . . is this lipstick, the color of my lipstick, all right? I've never worn this shade before.

MEG: It looks good on you. It's a good color for you.

JENNIFER: You think so? Really?

MEG: I do. [*Smiling.*] It's a good "choice."

JENNIFER: Thanks. I don't know. It felt like a scientist choice, I don't know why. Sometimes you just have to go with your gut. [MEG *nods, goes back to her pages.*]

JENNIFER: [*Worrying.*] Patti Scharer. Do you get the light thing? They won't expect us to understand that, do you think? Stopping light? They won't grill us about that.

MEG: Probably not.

JENNIFER: I don't know. I read for the part of a veterinarian and they acted like they expected me to know everything about a dog's digestive system. I just winged it, talked about heartworm. I've seen them. In a jar. [MEG *doesn't respond.*] It's not just about the money. Truth be known, I'm feeling kind of stuck. [*Pause.*] If he's eating in there, stuffing his mouth with California pizza, Koo-koo-charoo chicken . . . You said you've read for him?

MEG: I used to go out with him.

JENNIFER: [*Stunned.*] You went out with him? You went out with Ethan Shroeder? [MEG *nods.*]

JENNIFER: Ohmygod, I'm so sorry. What I said . . . I didn't mean to call him a monster. Maybe he was just . . . hungry when my friend read for him. Maybe he's perfectly—

MEG: It's okay. A lot of people think he's an asshole.

JENNIFER: They do. You're not going out with him any more? [**MEG** *shakes her head.*] You're still friends? I mean, you're okay reading for him?

MEG: I really like this part.

JENNIFER: [*Not really like it.*] You do?

MEG: I do. How often does that happen?

JENNIFER: Yeah. Really. You must like this part.

MEG: I find the subject fascinating. I've read quite a bit about it.

JENNIFER: Oh. So . . . Light travels a hundred and eighty thousand miles an hour . . .

MEG: A second.

JENNIFER: And . . . [**JENNIFER** *waits for* **MEG** *to explain it.*] Then they stop it in a jar. [*Thinking . . .*] Like heartworm. Preserve it in formaldehyde.

MEG: Chilled sodium gas, actually.

JENNIFER: It just hangs in there? Frozen?

MEG: Well, the light goes out. It gets fainter and fainter as it slows down. The most amazing part to me—it's all amazing—they can revive the light any time by flashing a second beam of light through the gas.

JENNIFER: Oh.

MEG: They can bring a beam of light to a full stop, hold it, and then send it on its way with a second beam. [*Pause.*]

JENNIFER: I like scenes best . . . when I can go deep. Cry. I like emotion. My background is theatre.

MEG: Not a lot of emotion in these scenes, not ostensibly.

JENNIFER: No. That's why I was thinking the French . . .

MEG: Go for the accent.

JENNIFER: You think so? [*Another actress enters. She is very appealing, made-up, a knock-out. She takes a seat. Exudes confidence. Both* MEG *and* JENNIFER *look at her, silently, as she takes out many pages and starts going through them.*]

PATTI: [*To* JENNIFER, *all business.*] Excuse me, are your pages with the reporter dated May eleventh or May fifteenth? [JENNIFER *looks at her pages . . .*]

JENNIFER: The reporter? I don't have . . . [JENNIFER *flips through, looking . . .*]

PATTI: Never mind. [*Noticing . . .*] Meg.

MEG: Hi, Patti.

PATTI: How *are* you? [MEG *nods, friendly, a little guarded.*]

PATTI: It's so great to see you, are you here now?

MEG: I'm here.

PATTI: You know I'd heard that. I ran into Carolyn, she was stage managing *Vanya* at the Taper, she told me you'd moved back.

MEG: I did.

PATTI: That's great. And you're reading for Ethan?

MEG: I am.

PATTI: Wow. Wow. [PATTI *studies MEG, waiting for some kind of response, which is not forthcoming.*]

MEG: How's Olivia?

PATTI: Olivia is three, God help me. Meg, can I borrow your lipstick, I actually forgot mine.

MEG: I'm sorry. I actually left all my makeup in the car.

PATTI: Really? What were you thinking? [PATTI *maintains her charming smile, miffed underneath.* JENNIFER *stares at* PATTI *in a mixed stupor of defeat and envy.*]

JENNIFER: [*Stirring.*] I have some lipstick. You can borrow.

PATTI: [*Brightly.*] Great. Thanks. [JENNIFER *reaches down into her purse and takes out her lipstick, takes off the cap, and offers it to* PATTI. PATTI, *looking at* JENNIFER's *lips:*] Oh. Is it the color you're wearing?

JENNIFER: Uh-huh.

PATTI: That's okay. That color . . . I can't wear that color. But, thanks. [*Mortified,* JENNIFER *looks down at the color, gradually retreats her hand, puts the cover back on and sticks the lipstick back in her purse. Pause as all study the script.*]

PATTI: [*To* MEG.] I admire you, Meg. I really do. Reading for Ethan. That takes guts.

MEG: Not really.

PATTI: The way he treated you. You know Carolyn's first A.D.

[MEG *nods.*] You know they're an item. Ethan and Carolyn. She's pregnant. That's ironic, huh? [MEG *did not know this. She flinches slightly. The door opens and* GEORGIA *enters with the casting agent behind her.* GEORGIA *grabs a sweater she left on a chair, waves to the* CASTING AGENT, *exiting.*]

CASTING AGENT: Thanks, Georgia. Patti. You made it.

PATTI: I'm so sorry I'm late. The 405 was a nightmare.

CASTING AGENT: You want to come in? Or do you want to take a minute. Jennifer . . . ? [JENNIFER, *discombobulated, jumps up, dropping all her pages as* PATTI *grabs her purse, coat, stands up.*]

PATTI: I'm fine. [PATTI *heads smoothly into the audition room. The* CASTING AGENT *smiles at* MEG, *looks down at the pages* JENNIFER *has dropped, and exits into the audition room.*]

JENNIFER: [*Crying, wiping her nose on her sleeve.*] I'm sorry. Do you have another tissue? [MEG *hands her another tissue which* JENNIFER *uses to wipe her nose and wipe away tears.* JENNIFER *grabs her stuff and hurries out.*]

JENNIFER: [*Not looking at* MEG.] It was very nice meeting you.

MEG: Where are you going?

JENNIFER: [*Crying, halfway out the door.*] I don't know. Bye.

MEG: Wait! [JENNIFER *turns and looks at her.*] You can get this part. [JENNIFER *is sobbing.*]

JENNIFER: I can't get this part.

MEG: You can.

JENNIFER: I can't. I can't even audition for this part.

MEG: Sit down.

JENNIFER: What?

MEG: Pull yourself together. Sit down.

JENNIFER: [*Weepy, discombobulated.*] Where?

MEG: On that chair. Go ahead. Sit! [JENNIFER *sits back down on her chair, sniffling.*] Here. Put these on. [MEG *takes the pair of tortoise-shell glasses she is wearing and gives them to* JENNIFER.] Put them on. [JENNIFER *does.*]

JENNIFER: Why does she want this part? It's not even very big.

MEG: Patti Scharer is not going to get this part.

JENNIFER: Yes, she is.

MEG: No she's not.

JENNIFER: [*Crying.*] She's already got it. She's already in there. With the part.

MEG: Ethan can't stand Patti Scharer. He's not going to give her this part. He's going to give you this part, because it's your part. [JENNIFER *pauses crying to look at her.*]

JENNIFER: He can't stand her?

MEG: Jennifer, listen to me. Light . . . is emotion. [JENNIFER, *somewhat calmer but still a mess, response to the intensity of* MEG*'s voice. Listens . . .*] Think of light, a beam of light . . . as a story, a story with its own past, its own history. The light has been who knows where, has illuminated who knows what. Maybe it's been traveling for a long, long time—decades, centuries. And somewhere along its journey, it starts to slow down . . . Take a pause, fold into itself . . . [*The lights on them start to dim . . .*] Okay, so . . . Now, I want you to imagine you're at the theatre. You're sitting in the audience, and you're watching a play. You say you love theatre?

JENNIFER: [*Blowing her nose.*] I do. Why are you doing this?

MEG: So the curtain has just opened, and there are three people on stage, and they're still, not moving. [*Lights keep dimming.*] Who are these people, these characters? What is their past? Their history? We don't know. At the beginning of the play, we don't know anything about them at all. Their pasts are frozen. Suspended. [*The lights stop dimming, and* **MEG** *and* **JENNIFER** *are still for a few moments, frozen, in close to dark.*] Then the play begins . . . [*Lights start to slowly fade up.*] . . . and we start to learn things about them. Information unfolds. One character leaves. Facts are revealed. We learn that this character really needs something, or this character has a dream, a passion, or maybe this one's been hurt . . . [*A spotlight lights her dimly and gets brighter slowly during the following . . .*] . . . been hurt really, really badly and we don't know how. Within minutes we can learn so much about them. In less than ten minutes, we can see the DNA of their whole lives. Even though there are mysteries, we feel we know them, quite well. Then, there comes that moment, that inevitable pivotal moment in a scene when things turn. The epiphany. The revelation. Something is illuminated. [*The spotlight on her is very bright now. Other lights are up to half full.*]

JENNIFER: I think . . . you're probably saying something but I'm not sure what it is. [**MEG** *looks at her. Takes the barrette out of her hair.*]

MEG: I think you should put your hair back. Here, take my barrette. [**MEG** *hand her barrette to* **JENNIFER**, *who puts her hair back.*] That's good. You look . . . like a scientist.

JENNIFER: What did Ethan Schroeder do to you that was so bad? [**MEG** *takes a moment to answer.*]

MEG: Nothing terribly original. [MEG *goes to get her things to leave.*]

JENNIFER: You're not going to read for this part?

MEG: No.

JENNIFER: One thing . . . I do feel emotional, right now. [*A spotlight on* JENNIFER *starts to come up, as all other lights start to fade, including the spotlight on* MEG.] For you, mainly.

MEG: Use it. Hold it inside. And, I would suggest you drop the accent.

JENNIFER: Really?

MEG: You don't need it. Another thing . . . when you go in there, tell Ethan he looks like a young Richard Burton.

JENNIFER: Okay. I can do that. I can do that.

MEG: This is your part. [*All lights are out now except the spotlight on* JENNIFER.]

JENNIFER: [*Confidently, seriously looking like a scientist.*] I know. This is my part. This is my part. [*The spotlight on* JENNIFER *is up to full. Then it fades out.*]

A BODY OF WATER

by Neena Beber

CHARACTERS:

Marguerite

Joe

NOTE: Marguerite and Joe are in their teens, but project themselves into their futures. Or they are old, and recalling themselves in their youth. They can be played by old or young actors, or in any combination concocted by the artists involved. In the HB production the piece was performed twice, at the suggestion of artistic director Billy Carden: with young actors at the beginning of the evening, and older ones at the end. The staging was changed slightly to suggest the implications of the repetition, the looking forward followed by the looking back on the same event. It was directed at HB by Lindsay Firman.

NEENA BEBER'S plays include *The Dew Point, Jump/Cut, Hard Feelings, A Common Vision, Tomorrowland, The Brief but Exemplary Life of the Living Goddess, Failure to Thrive,* the one-act *Misreading,* and the children's play *Zachariah Moseley's Neon Blues.* Some of the theatres that have premiered her work: Woolly Mammoth, Theatre J, The Magic Theatre, The Women's Project, Gloucester Stage, New Georges, Padua Hills Playwrights Festival, The Humana Festival, and Arielle Tepper's Summer Play Festival. She has received an L. Arnold Weissberger Award for Playwriting, an A.S.K. Exchange to The Royal Court Theatre in London, a MacDowell Colony Fellowship, grants from AT&T and the NEA, and commissions from Playwrights Horizon, Otterbein College, and The Magic Theater. *Jump/Cut* was a Finalist for the Susan Smith Blackburn Prize and was nominated for a Helen Hayes Award for Outstanding New Play.

Ms. Beber is a member of New Dramatists, The New York Playwrights Lab, HB Playwrights Unit, and The Women's Project.

MARGUERITE *and* JOE, *reclining.*

MARGUERITE: I look fat. Do I look fat?

JOE: No.

MARGUERITE: Look at me. I'm so fat. This bathing suit makes me look fat. Admit it. I'm, like, totally bloated. I just—uchh—it's disgusting.

JOE: You're not fat.

MARGUERITE: [*Off unseen passerby.*] Do I look like that? I look like that, right?

JOE: You spend too much time focusing on the physical.

MARGUERITE: Well it's the beach. We're at the beach.

JOE: I'll bet you spend 80% of your waking time focused on your physical presence in the world. Does it matter? Will it? Ultimately?

MARGUERITE: Are you saying this because I look fat? [*She stands and steps forward.*] Years later I develop a conscience, a strong moral fiber, an interest in social justice. I march for human rights, I march against fur, I march for humanitarian efforts abroad, I march against hunger, I march for the environment, I march for Palestinians, Bosnians, Hindus, Pakistanis, Sri Lankans, Peruvians, Christians, non-believers, Jews; I chain myself to a tree, to a wall, to a tractor; I am sent to prison for a short time, I am stabbed in prison, I survive, the scar gets darker over time before it fades. [*Goes back to sunning; of her own flesh:*] This should not be here. I'm supposed to be in the prime of my youth, the full bloom or whatever. Most people don't even have to exercise until they're way into their like twenties or something, and look at me, I'm already—I hate this.

JOE: This is why it makes sense to cover. Not just to protect you from the temptation of others, but to protect you from the temptation from yourself to think only of surfaces. To protect yourself from the judgment of others and of yourself. A physical barrier frees you from physical limitations.

MARGUERITE: You're saying this because I look fat. Are you? [*Observing someone else.*] Some people look really good in bathing suits and some people don't. [*He says nothing, staring off.*] It's not like your thoughts are so deep. I mean, are you even going to go to college, Joe?

JOE: [*Back on mat.*] Not everyone gets to go to college.

MARGUERITE: But you're smart. You could.

JOE: Well gee, thanks, but you're not the one who makes the decisions. I don't think you understand how things work. The tides—do you even understand how the tides work?

MARGUERITE: I don't know. Gravity. Or something. The full moon?

JOE: There are forces bigger than us, that's all I'm saying. [*Stepping forward.*] Years later I return to the Germany of my grandparents. I am searching for the synagogue where my grandfather prayed. I am searching for the marzipan factory. I am searching for the ancestral home. Years later I have this need to return to a place I never knew. [*Back, to* MARGUERITE.] Do you want to go in the water?

MARGUERITE: You're so skinny.

JOE: I'm not skinny.

MARGUERITE: I wish I were skinny like you.

JOE: Guys don't exactly want to get called "skinny" if you want to get into that. Which I don't. [*Looking off at water.*] I really like the beach. I like to come here and think. Don't ruin that for me. I like to watch the waves.

MARGUERITE: There aren't even any waves today. No big ones, anyway, none you can ride. It's so calm. [*Stepping forward.*] Years later, I find myself at a train station after my divorce, which is bitter and protracted. I have an existential crisis. I travel widely. I come to understand my mother. [*Not knowing why:*] Years later, I cry at such simple things. [*Back.*] Are you going to try to ride the waves today? Joe? [*No response.*] I'll bet your thoughts aren't that deep. I'll bet underneath it all they aren't any deeper than mine.

JOE: I miss the beach.

MARGUERITE: How can you miss it when we're right here?

JOE: I don't know. [*Stepping forward.*] Years later I develop arthritis, diverticulitus, gallstones, mild diabetes, and an enlarged prostate. I pee night and day and I can't take a shit. I have an affair with a younger woman. Her skin is so plain and smooth that I weep.

MARGUERITE: [*Observing someone else:*] God. I hope I don't get that old. I can't imagine it. Can you imagine—us? No way. They'll probably have things they can do to keep it all together by then, right?

JOE: You might want to protect yourself from the elements. If you care. I don't. But you might not want to be out here if you care so much about the wrapper so to speak.

MARGUERITE: I hate growing up in a beach community. It's a lot of pressure, you know? At this age. I liked being a little girl and not thinking about it.

JOE: You're still young and you know it. And you know you're not fat. You know it. You know you're fucking perfect, Marguerite.

MARGUERITE: Little kids are perfect. And they don't have to think about it. It never comes up. They just don't.

JOE: I'm going to go in.

MARGUERITE: Did you say perfect? Do you really think that? Joe?
[*He looks back at her, wanting to kiss her. He doesn't muster the nerve.*]

JOE: [*Forward.*] Years later I find myself at the Dead Sea, where it takes little effort to float. Years later I float for hours on the Dead Sea. I float. I float. I float.

MARGUERITE: [*Forward.*] Years later I long to return / to the water / to the heat / to the hard pillows of sand / to that feeling / that feeling that you get only from the ocean / and the air like this/ the way it smells / the stickiness the saltiness the heat— / My room is small and far from the ocean but I long to return / to this. [JOE *runs toward the water.*]

MARGUERITE: Are you going in? I'll bet you there are jelly fish. Did you hear me? Joe? Jelly fish, the kind that sting.

JOE: [*Already apart from her, almost off.*] I'm going in. Come on. Come on in, Marguerite. [*They go into the ocean. Blackout, end of play.*]

HELP

by Neena Beber

CHARACTERS:

Beverly

Gina

PLACE:

Two women at a long folding table
in an institutional setting.

NOTE: This play was originally presented by Urban Empire; artistic
director: Jack Merril, director: Rachel Dickstein.

NEENA BEBER'S plays include *The Dew Point, Jump/Cut, Hard
Feelings, A Common Vision, Tomorrowland, The Brief but Exemplary
Life of the Living Goddess, Failure to Thrive,* the one-act *Misreading,*
and the children's play *Zachariah Moseley's Neon Blues.* Some of the
theatres that have premiered her work: Woolly Mammoth, Theatre J,
The Magic Theatre, The Women's Project, Gloucester Stage, New
Georges, Padua Hills Playwrights Festival, The Humana Festival, and
Arielle Tepper's Summer Play Festival. She has received an L. Arnold
Weissberger Award for Playwriting, an A.S.K. Exchange to The Royal
Court Theatre in London, a MacDowell Colony Fellowship, grants
from AT&T and the NEA, and commissions from Playwrights Horizon,
Otterbein College, and The Magic Theater. *Jump/Cut* was a Finalist for
the Susan Smith Blackburn Prize and was nominated for a Helen Hayes
Award for Outstanding New Play.

Ms. Beber is a member of New Dramatists, The New York
Playwrights Lab, HB Playwrights Unit, and The Women's Project.

BEVERLY: It's really very simple. You set the table with these paper plates. The cups are over here. We use real cutlery except for the knives, which have to be plastic. We're having chicken tonight, it's warming in the oven. Smell? Ah, yes. We've got two kinds of salads, potato and macaroni. They'll tell you what they want. They can help themselves to the green salad. The coffee is on. Water and soda over there.

GINA: Do I serve it from here?

BEVERLY: That's right, they'll hand you their plate and you'll fill it.

GINA: I don't do anything else?

BEVERLY: You'll clean up after. The bus drops them off at seven or so. They'll set up their beds in the other rooms first.

GINA: Do we help with the beds?

BEVERLY: Most of the people we get are regulars, they already know the routine. "Guests" we call them, more humane. You haven't done this before?

GINA: No, I . . . not exactly, no. I've meant to. I've done other kinds of things, delivering meals, coat drives and so on.

BEVERLY: Oh, no, dear, I wasn't testing your munificence, I simply wondered if you'd volunteered at a soup kitchen before.

GINA: God, I'm so . . . it's just that I've always meant to do more. No, I haven't. How many places do I set?

BEVERLY: Let's see, it should be eleven tonight.

GINA: Only eleven?

BEVERLY: You were hoping for more?

GINA: No, no, I wouldn't put it that way, no.

BEVERLY: You sounded so disappointed. "Only eleven?"

GINA: I meant if there *are* more out there *already* it would be nice if we could, you know, feed more. As long as we're at it.

BEVERLY: We like to keep the program small. Less impersonal.

GINA: That's nice. I just—I feel like I have so little to do.

BEVERLY: You'll eat. We eat with our guests. Is that a problem for you?

GINA: Of course not. I just hate to waste the food on ourselves.

BEVERLY: We all need to eat. We're all equals here, that's part of the philosophy. You need to eat as much as anyone else. I hope you haven't eaten yet. Sitting with them, that's part of it. Do you like chicken?

GINA: I'm a vegetarian, but . . . the salads look great.

BEVERLY: It would be better if you could eat the chicken. We don't want it to look like it's not good enough for us.

GINA: Oh, no, of course that's not it, I . . . I'll just eat it, that's all.

BEVERLY: It feels good helping people, doesn't it?

GINA: Yes, it does. Very much so. [*Beat.*] I haven't had chicken in ages. So I was just wondering, what time do you think I'll be finished here? When I called, they didn't tell me, and, um . . .

BEVERLY: Are you in a hurry?

GINA: Not at all. Well, I am meeting some people afterwards, so if it's going to go late, I should make a call, that's all. But I'm happy to stay as long as necessary. I want to stay.

BEVERLY: It shouldn't be more than an hour once they get here. Counting cleaning up. The guests don't tend to socialize much.

GINA: Oh. Well see there? I thought it would be much longer than an hour.

BEVERLY: There you go sounding disappointed again.

GINA: That's not it, I just . . . I wish I could do more.

BEVERLY: As long as you're here.

GINA: Well, yes. I've tried to come before, but they get overbooked on holidays.

BEVERLY: We can get a few too many volunteers. As you can see, there really isn't that much to do. The food's already prepared.

GINA: Have you been volunteering here for a while?

BEVERLY: I'm on most nights. Of course it's too bad we only help eleven. Sometimes twelve.

GINA: It does seem like a very small number.

BEVERLY: You probably passed eleven homeless beggars on your way over here alone. Where do you live?

GINA: Downtown. West Village.

BEVERLY: Eleven on the subway alone, am I right?

GINA: I took a cab. Actually. I don't usually. I was running late.

BEVERLY: A cab from downtown? That must have cost quite a bit in this traffic.

GINA: It wasn't that bad. It's not far. God, it does seem ridiculous in this situation, doesn't it?

BEVERLY: And you'll want to cab it home. To be safe.

GINA: I usually do take the subway. Or walk. I try not to take cabs, believe me, but when I saw I was running late . . .

BEVERLY: The cab driver has to make a living, too. Someone has to be willing to spring for it or what would they do.

GINA: That's true.

BEVERLY: I'm sure you tip well.

GINA: [*Tense.*] Shall I set the cups, or leave them by the soda?

BEVERLY: Go ahead and set them. Don't think I'm staring at your feet, but I'm quite admiring those shoes.

GINA: Really? Thank you.

BEVERLY: May I touch?

GINA: They're nothing special.

BEVERLY: I'd love to see the ones you consider special.

GINA: I didn't mean it that way—

BEVERLY: They look exceptionally well made. But of course you've chosen to dress in a fairly subdued, unobtrusive way. That was very thoughtful of you, Gina.

GINA: But I always dress this way. I'm just wearing my usual clothes.

BEVERLY: Not too done, I like that. Simple. Elegant. Good quality. I know clothes. I used to work in the garment industry. Many years ago. Lifetimes ago.

GINA: You don't look that old. I mean, at all old.

BEVERLY: That's kind of you to say, Gina. Are you involved with someone?

GINA: Am I—

BEVERLY: Boyfriend, girlfriend? I take it you're not married. I'm only asking because a lot of young women seem to come here hoping Mr. Wonderful, Mr. Do-Gooder, will be standing beside them serving soup and he's also a millionaire investment banker. Isn't that a hoot?

GINA: It's not my intention to meet someone. I'm perfectly satisfied in that department, thank you. Do you think the chicken is ready?

BEVERLY: It's better to keep it warm. It's chilly in here, no?

GINA: A little. I didn't want to complain.

BEVERLY: There's a draft. Drafty wafty. Not as cold as outside, at least, but I am chilly.

GINA: Would you like to borrow my scarf?

BEVERLY: Is it cashmere? [*Taking the scarf.*] Oh, yes, I can tell—mmm, I *would* like to borrow it.

GINA: Please.

BEVERLY: [*Maybe joking.*] In fact, I'd like to keep it.

GINA: [*Maybe joking.*] *You're* not homeless, now.

BEVERLY: If I were, would you let me keep the scarf? Because we can give it to one of the eleven—that's what we'll do. But how will we choose? It will seem so unfair, to select one to receive the scarf while the others must go without. Maybe we can cut it into two scarves; four even, it's awfully long and lush—

GINA: I'm not giving my scarf away, dammit.

BEVERLY: Oh. I see. I apologize. I really shouldn't give you a hard time. You've probably dropped off six bag-fuls at Goodwill just this week. Probably some scarves in there.

GINA: Yes, there were.

BEVERLY: Not as nice as this one, maybe; this isn't what gets allotted to the Goodwill pile.

GINA: I gave away some very nice things. Just as nice.

BEVERLY: But you happen to be particularly fond of this one.

GINA: That's right. Oh, just forget it. Keep it, or—whatever. I don't want it back. I won't be able to enjoy wearing it again anyway.

BEVERLY: Nonsense, it's an excellent color for you. You must wear it and enjoy it and never think "if you don't have for all, don't give at all." But oh, someone *did* give it to you and no one gave me one; or did you buy it for yourself?

GINA: Do you have a problem with me, Mrs. Winn?

BEVERLY: Beverly, please. What kind of a problem do you have in mind, Gina?

GINA: I get the feeling you don't like me. You seem somewhat suspicious. Of my motivation coming here. From the moment I arrived, you've been . . . you've been acting like I'm wrong to come here, to have signed up. Yes, I'm here because I wanted to help in some way. Because it makes me feel good to help. And because I have a kind of guilt, yes, about what I've been given. If you're looking for a different kind of motive, please, let me know.

BEVERLY: I think you're overreacting. I was just trying to get to know you, Gina; where you're coming from and all that.

GINA: No, you seem to think it's wrong to want to do good. Well, what if we were to stop? What if none of us wanted to contribute on anything less than a grand scale? Your little soup kitchen would have to close up shop like that. Everyone must do a little, even a little, and if we all—

BEVERLY: There you go, Gina; there you go, my girl. And if we can't teach them to fish because we haven't *that* much time, or energy, or resources, we will give them the fish, dammit—at least we will give them the fish.

GINA: People do need to eat. Better to eat for a day than not at all.

BEVERLY: Bravo, I'm with you all the way. Much better than the last fellow we had, he said he volunteered to be assured safe passage on the airplane he was taking the next day.

GINA: Screw that. The good die every single second of every single minute, the self-righteous fool.

BEVERLY: That's right, life's not a swap meet. And screw those arrogant, ignorant sons-of-bitches who say, "If I can make it, anyone can."

GINA: I hate that, yes. You can't imagine who said something just like that to me once—a blind date I had, and he was a very wealthy guy I might add. Wouldn't give money to a beggar, this poor guy was rooting through garbage for cans.

BEVERLY: "Hey, if I did it—"

GINA: Exactly, as if he didn't have everything going for him.

BEVERLY: Couldn't get the guy to spring for a quarter, eh?

GINA: Not even.

BEVERLY: But maybe it isn't the right thing to do. Maybe he'll spend it on drugs. On boozy woozy, on crack or smack, on—

GINA: Not you, too, Beverly. The man was digging in the garbage. It was nasty. He was desperate.

BEVERLY: I wonder if he ever found his way here, do you think?

GINA: Well, I . . . I don't know, Beverly.

BEVERLY: Maybe you'll recognize him. Probably not, though; you probably walked by very quickly, so how could you—well, too bad for him. We have some of the nicest cots in the system—thick mattresses. This is one of the better shelters—you're a lucky bum to get assigned here.

GINA: It does seem . . . clean.

BEVERLY: I know about the system. I was in it for years. Does that surprise you?

GINA: I didn't realize.

BEVERLY: I'm barely out now. I'm just hanging on by the hair on my chinny chin chin, if you know what I'm saying.

GINA: You seem to be doing very well.

BEVERLY: I'm finally over the drug addiction. Caffeine. Don't look at me that way: a six-dollar-a-day cappuccino habit can really put you over the edge when you're already teetering, am I right?

GINA: It does add up.

BEVERLY: Don't you just love those three-dollar frothy cappuccinos with real chocolate sprinkles? I know I couldn't do without, I just couldn't; I was up to nearly fifty dollars a week on the things, multiply that by fifty-two, that's two-thousand six-hundred every year on my god-damned cappuccinos. I miss those sweethearts. I really should have invested in a machine of my own after a point, but then, where would I put it? Not the kind of thing you can lug around in a shopping cart very easily.

GINA: That must have been awful for you.

BEVERLY: Don't worry, most of the people who come here are much nicer than me. They don't blame you.

GINA: Well, um, why would they blame me?

BEVERLY: Hold on, Gina, hold on. See, they might covet those nice shoes you have on your little feet, but generally that's not on their minds. Some of them might lust for a piece of that pretty pink flesh of yours, but generally that's not on their minds either, believe it or not. They're tired, real tired, and happy enough to get a bite of macaroni salad and a warm bed for the night. They don't blame you for their situation at all. They know that even if you're not, well, "political," your heart is in the right place; you vote for all the right candidates. Except when you once-in-a-while don't manage to get to the polls in time but damn, you feel so bad about it afterwards, who could hold it against you? And besides, you tell yourself that they're all alike anyway, lousy politicians, so what does it matter. We see all that, Gina, and understand your good nature, your generous heart; hell, we'd spend four hundred bucks on a pair of shoes, too, if we could.

GINA: That's an outrageously exaggerated—I bought these on sale, and you're—you're being very unfair.

BEVERLY: Unfair? What a brilliant word. There's so much of it going around these days.

GINA: Yes. You're right. I'm so sorry.

BEVERLY: I'm trying to say that I understand, Gina; what's a girl supposed to do? I know because I was just like you, dear. Don't look alarmed. Of course, a few of those fluffy layers you've got to cushion the fall were sorely lacking in my case; I had the job for a while but no man with the job, no mommy to come to the rescue "till you get back on your feet, hon"; no daddy with the charge card "to use in emergencies, sweet pea"; no health care insurance when needed; plus a small bit of mental instability that tends to run in my family when things get absolutely smack down to the bottom of the barrel and your whole world falls apart like you never thought it could. [GINA *is shivering, just a little;* BEVERLY *gives her back her scarf;* GINA *begins to wrap it around herself like a cocoon.*] But I'm sure most people have that tendency; how would they know, right? They needn't ever know. You see, a lot of things have to go wrong all at once. So don't worry, you probably won't end up where I did. It's highly unlikely. Anyway, dear, there's always someone's who's got it worse, so you mustn't let the guilt run wild because you've got it better, if you know what I mean. [*An oven timer bell goes off.*] Oh, the chickens are ready. Our guests will be here any second. Gina? Dear? Don't you want to help? [GINA *clutches the scarf in her hand, drops it by her feet. She looks down at her shoes. She is frozen in place, helpless. Bright lights and then blackout.*]

DEFUSION
by Brooke Berman

CHARACTERS:

A Woman

A Man

BROOKE BERMAN'S *The Triple Happiness* recently premiered at
Second Stage Theatre in New York City and was developed through
ASK, The Royal Court Theatre, The Playwrights Center in Minneapolis,
and Hourglass Theatre in New York City. Her play *Until We Find Each
Other* premiered at Steppenwolf Theatre Company in Chicago and was
workshopped at the O'Neill Center. Ms. Berman's short play *Dancing
with a Devil* (co-winner of the Heideman Award at Actors Theatre of
Louisville in 1999) was presented as part of the Humana Festival and
received an American Theater Critics Best New Play nomination.

Ms. Berman has received numerous awards and fellowships for
her writing, including a Berilla Kerr Foundation grant (2002), Helen
Merrill Award (2000), Francesca Primus Award (1998, 2000), Lila
Acheson Wallace American Playwrights Fellowship at the Juilliard
School, Lecomte du Nouy Award (1998 and 1999), an Independent
Artist Challenge grant, and a commissioning grant from the National
Foundation for Jewish Culture. She is a graduate of The Juilliard
School and a resident playwright of New Dramatists.

WOMAN: It starts with a walk. [*Lights up on* **WOMAN.**] It is the night before New Year's Eve and we walk through an alleyway in the dark to your car. I know you, sort of, not well. You are an acquaintance in the classic sense. I knew you slightly, once, sort of, when I was seventeen and wore no shoes. It is ten years after being 17 when I call you on business. You work in my field, and I am looking for something. Inspiration, maybe, or a job. I have suggested we meet as I will be in your city for the day to see an old friend, and it all works out so well. I take a cab from the train station to your office. You are friendly and enthusiastic. There is something we might call chemistry, perhaps, although I am not calling it that.

We are in your city, not mine. We will always be in your city, not mine. I do not know, in the moment that we will call now, that there will be such a context as "always". I do not know much. Including my way around. I follow your lead. You are everything my mother would approve of. The Nice Jewish Girl I rarely admit to responds almost alchemically, or hormonally, to the Nice Jewish Boy in you, and there is this thing I am not calling chemistry. But I enjoy the walk between your office and the car.

MAN: I remember the walk. I do not remember it as the night before the New Year. I don't know when it was. But I do remember the walk and the ice. There was ice, and it was slippery. And, years later, I will ask you about that walk and wonder when it happened because the walk is already synonymous with the moment the question first began to take shape.

WOMAN: The question is not yet a question. It will become one later, with multiple choice and essay options.

MAN: The walk ends with a drive, and I deposit you at your friend's dad's house on the other side of town. Near the museum. A part of town I, parenthetically, like quite a bit. And I like this drive. What did we talk about?

WOMAN: I don't remember. But, you bring me to the door (those Nice Jewish Boy manners of yours) and I think the non-question in a non-way, and I forget all about you, really. There is dinner, after all, and a long train ride home on the commuter train and not Amtrak because it is cheaper this way but takes all day. It is New Years' Eve. Or did I already mention that?

MAN: And three years pass. Just pass.

WOMAN: Until now. It is three years later, and I am unemployed and in love with my boyfriend, a 25-year-old vegetarian chef. He feeds me but cannot make a commitment. I eat well and wait. We don't live together, though he keeps saying that in about six months, he will be ready. I think that in his mind six months is a very long time. He acquires a pot-smoking habit, which makes him boring, forgetful, unreliable and sometimes asexual. We are told that men who smoke large quantities of pot run the risk of decreased sex drive, and sperm count, and this worries me, not to mention the fact that even when he isn't stoned, pot brings out a kind of Beavis and Butthead quality that I find troublesome. One Friday night, he and his friends trip on nutmeg (which apparently produces a psychedelic experience on the level of acid, lasting for many days, should one ingest large enough portions) and he calls me at 2 AM from a payphone in Times Square apparently having what is called a bad trip.

MAN: But, you see, you are at home on that Friday night, computer on, modem connected, indulging in a little email adultery with me.

WOMAN: This starts innocently enough. A revival of our old professional, sort of personal, again superficial, past. I have contacted you by—telephone perhaps? a note?

MAN: I believe you sent a note. And I called. I asked about your work. How is your work?

WOMAN: You suggest I email, and you give me the address. We exchange digital hellos, and then you ask me what my favorite flavor ice cream is and if no such flavor exists, and I could design my own, what might that be—

MAN: It is a good question.

WOMAN: Clearly—because I have a lot of thoughts on this topic. I am tired of sending my boyfriend out for sweets and being disappointed when he comes back with vanilla. Who comes back with vanilla when there are flavors that contain large masses of chocolate and peanut butter and mocha? And this is how you get in. You like the large masses too. You like chocolate. You enter, unseen and smoothly, through a hole in the ozone layer, through the space where my boyfriend has boring taste.

MAN: We email each other daily, sometimes twice daily, for two weeks.

WOMAN: Since I am spending a great deal of my unemployed time at home trying to avoid spending money, this correspondence takes on an importance. It is free. And you are charming. You move into the foreground of what interests me, while my boyfriend is tripping on seemingly innocent kitchen spices and making sure I know he is not ready to settle down. I look forward to you, to our contact, daily, and this takes the edge off all those places where the edges are sharp and cut me and leave shards of glass in places they should not. You enter. There is room.

You are lonely. You do not say as much, but it is there, nonetheless, in your tone and your eagerness to flirt. Maybe I can say this because I am lonely too and it takes one to know one. We remember things about one another, even though we were really day players and not leads in one another's' pasts. The walk. A canvas schoolbag you once owned. The way I used to talk about past lives.

MAN: When you were 17 and wore no shoes.

WOMAN: Right. I don't remember that somehow, but I believe you.

MAN: It gets dangerous when I come home looking forward to hearing from you. Like a bedtime story. Or a habit. Or love. I want to be faithful to you. And I haven't seen you in three years, and before that in ten.

WOMAN: At the risk of sounding like the Nora Ephron movie, I too am coming home breathless, wondering if I've got mail.

MAN: This is a form of courtship.

WOMAN: Yes. It is. Your emails have a startling and immediate physical effect on me.

MAN: Really?

WOMAN: "I have a boyfriend, you know." I make sure that you do know, once I am sure that we are flirting. A boyfriend who, (parenthetically) has the same first name as you.

MAN: How odd. I mean don't you find that odd?

WOMAN: Maybe. It reminds me of a joke my mother used to tell about moaning someone's name in a moment of passion, but I never found the joke funny, so there is that.

MAN: I see.

WOMAN: You are what he is not. Namely, 35, Jewish, and highly educated, with a sense of humor which indicates that you have read and appropriately marveled at J.D. Salinger. (I am thinking here most especially of Franny and Zooey, or perhaps the Esme story, although we have never discussed any of this outright.)

MAN: We look at our options.

WOMAN: We discuss geography and desire.

MAN: You should come here.

WOMAN: A visit. At your house and not mine as there is the issue of two roommates and a boyfriend. My apartment is not amenable to sin or even walking around naked.

MAN: You should really come here.

WOMAN: So, your house it is. You offer me a weekend with you, to see what will happen, like a science experiment, when we are in the same city, the same room, when we are in physical proximity. You are a man. A real man. A grown up. I like this. You know what you want, and I think you think you want me. You say, "I have to make this real."

MAN: I do. Real, and not virtual. I'll pay for your ticket.

WOMAN: You say, "I can live no more by thinking"

MAN: Quoting William Shakespeare. Orlando in "As You Like It."

WOMAN: . . . which hits a nerve you do not know about. You see, I am someone who can be wooed by literature.

MAN: Which means?

WOMAN: William Shakespeare is scoring you points.

MAN: Good.

WOMAN: This is when the question first takes on multiple choice format. I say, "these are what I see as our options," (a.) we keep emailing, don't meet, keep it safe. (b.) we meet, have great sex, no one gets hurt. (c.) we meet, fall in love and get married. Have a child. I name her Lucy. (d.) we meet and don't like each other at all and don't have great sex, or babies or anything. (e.) we work together. Sex optional. Still no one gets hurt.

MAN: (a.) is not an option. We have to meet. And I too have considered (b.) through (d.) —Isn't that funny? I have even considered marriage and children, though I might not name her Lucy. I might call her Boo. Or Whatever. And, actually, I can imagine other permutations but we can discuss that later. Come here.

WOMAN: You say, Come here. To see what happens in person.

MAN: In real time with real audio.

WOMAN: Oh. . . . I say, "I don't have the right clothes for an affair on your answering machine, because now I have passed into an entirely new realm of communication, the telephone. . . . And I cross my fingers and hold my breath and draw a Rune for guidance. The Rune says "the opposite of joy" so I draw another, and the second forecasts destruction and breakage. I draw them hourly waiting for the one that will sanction this trip. "I love my boyfriend." I say this all the time to everyone. But, the question between you and I has now been asked. And I am consumed with the desire to know / what will happen— / between us. The Runes forecast "events totally outside your control." I decide in the shower not to go. And then I pack. You say, we can go slow.

MAN: We can. I don't even <u>have</u> sex on the first date. Not anymore. I'm too old for that. You may not even kiss me.

WOMAN: But we both know I will kiss you.

MAN: Yes. We both know you will kiss me.

WOMAN: I tell him, my boyfriend with your name, that I will be away on business. I do not say it is the business of love and sex. I stop, on the way to the train, and compulsively buy black underwear at K-Mart. The trip takes me an hour and a half South to the City of Brotherly Love (and not of Infidelity and Deceit). I think "the only way to have "true love" is to be true yourself to love." I am thinking of him, not you, and I am not being true. I think, "I do not want to be untrue." I think, "This is just wrong" because I am not being true to anyone, not to him and also not to you, showing up with baggage and a boyfriend. And the train keeps moving South. When I stop in the train bathroom to put on my new black bra and g-string panties, I understand that there is a miscommunication between the part of me which does not wish to be outside of moral integrity and the part of me that is already swelling thinking about you.

Oh, my.

You meet my train, and I feel like a mail-order bride. I wonder if you will be disappointed.

MAN: But I'm not.

WOMAN: And you say, "Just so you know, it's all been de-fused," and this pierces my heart.

MAN: Listen, just so you know. It's all been defused.

WOMAN: What do you mean defused? Do you mean DE-FUSED or DIFFUSED?

MAN: The former.

WOMAN: Well. Should I turn around and go home?

MAN: No, of course not. I mean, of course not.

WOMAN: . . . and I do not go home.

MAN: I take you to one of the only places that serves dinner this time of night, and there are candles. We drink wine and talk about our lives.

WOMAN: We weave little pieces of our stories in and out and through, and then you take me to your house (you have a house!) and defused though you may be, you undress me on your plush red couch and make me feel like liquid and make me feel like joy, and not its opposite.

MAN: From the red couch we move upstairs to the bedroom, your new bra somewhere on my floor.

WOMAN: You have a bed, a real bed and not a futon. And there are kisses, and then you insist on reading something from George Bernard Shaw—

MAN: "Man and Superman."

WOMAN: You want to read *now?*—I find this weird but endearing, and I make you laugh and you make me come, and it is all very good. Except that you tire of my ambivalence about fidelity—

MAN: There are three of us in this bed.

WOMAN: I don't think there are three of us—

MAN: Your boyfriend is getting in my way.

WOMAN: —and you fall asleep on the other side of the bed that is big enough to have another side, our affair left slightly incomplete, if you know what I mean. This is when I suffer. It is the middle of the night and pangs of guilt start to shoot into and through me. And not just guilt, but remorse. And not just remorse, but fantasy. My boyfriend dissolves. I imagine making love to you in this bed on a regular basis, meeting you at the end of the day, writing in this house while you are gone. I get as far as dressing the kids in snowsuits when I start to feel really sick. I am not sick with fear of this reality, but rather, with my surprising longing for it. And this is the other thing. I know that you are not in love with me. And during the email phase, I thought you might be. But now I know you are not and will not ever, probably, be. You are asleep on the far side of your nice bed, in your own hemisphere. And I miss how my boyfriend and I sleep together—curled up inside one another. I fit perfectly in between all the folds of his legs and torso. He contains me. I fit. So I sit up and wonder / in your big soft bed /

why am i here?? I reach over and try to touch you, and you pull away.

MAN: In the morning I say, "If you were available, I would be scared."

WOMAN: And I say, "I'm going to go home today."

MAN: —even though our original plan was the weekend.

WOMAN: But, this is stupid and I miss my boyfriend who has your name.

MAN: So I agree to take you to the train. After we spend a day together in my city doing the things we would do if we were a we. If we were "we" together.

WOMAN: So we do all these things—

MAN: And then I take you to the train.

WOMAN: And I kiss you goodbye. Sweet. You taste like clove cigarettes and tobacco and it's sweet. And the floor is dropping, the ground, the bottom falling out from underneath me. This is what the Runes were warning me against. This feeling. This. [*Train sound/lights.*] Joy's antonym. Despair? Not—joy? Finally, I fall asleep.

MAN: After this, we do not email for awhile, the joy taken out of the discourse.

WOMAN: Joy's antonym.

MAN: The reverse, the opposite. I don't know. I don't really think about you much to be honest. I just don't think about it at all.

WOMAN: I think about it. But, there is more drama, more anti-joy, on its way. I spend Thanksgiving weekend watching *The Philadelphia Story* at home by myself and trying to become an alcoholic, which doesn't pan out at all because I fall asleep after the second glass of wine. Once the holiday passes, my boyfriend with your name confesses to adulterous activity of his own. On the exact same day that I was in your city with you. He says that he did it to prove to himself that he still could.

MAN: Oh, yeah I've done that.

WOMAN: I do not understand this at all. Anyway, I'm pretty calm, but I tell him: (a.) that you exist. (b.) that I have kissed you, and (c.) that I missed him.

MAN: (a.) I certainly exist, but (b.) you did more than kiss me, and (c.) I'm sorry.

WOMAN: [*Shrugs.*] It's okay. We break up six weeks after the trip to see you. I email and tell you all about. I don't know what I'm expecting, but what I am not expecting is—

MAN: I'm sorry to hear about you and the guy with my name. I hope you are okay. These things are tricky, are they not? My own life has taken an interesting turn. I'm getting back together with my ex-girlfriend. You don't know her. She is very nice.

WOMAN: Indeed. And, she does not share my name. I don't know what her name is, but I know it isn't the same as mine. And this reunion is a twist of fate, isn't that what they call it? I mean, the timing is really quite flawless. We will always be unavailable for each other, you and me. I date a bit. No one memorable. I kiss a punk rock musician with black nail polish. Mostly to see if I can. I wait for Spring, which I always like to believe will hold renewal. Or fusion, to fuse these elements of expectation that have been wrenched apart. I wonder how long before heartbreak stops hurting. I look for rebounding, but avoid it when it comes too close. There is this matter of the Spring coming. And walks I will take over the bridge and into the City and through parks and perhaps back to the West, which is the land of death and letting go. Death and letting go.

ALL
WE CAN
HANDLE

by Andrew Dainoff

CHARACTERS:

David

NOTE: When the dialogue is [between brackets] it emanates
from the unseen individual with whom David is conversing.

ANDREW DAINOFF lives in New York City, where the distractions are
immense. With the help of a fantastic group of friends, co-workers,
family, lovers, and an exceptional therapist, he bickers with the demons
that stop him from writing. He graduated from the fiction program at
Miami University in his hometown of Oxford, Ohio. Professors Eric
Goodman, John Romano, and Jim Reiss were helpful to his progress,
along with: Bill Cosby, David Mamet, Neal LaBute, Wallace Shawn,
Andre Dubus, Catherine Wadkins, Liza Lentini, Lajos Egri, Ricky
Gervais, Stephen Merchant, and his mother, Joyce. His play *All We
Can Handle* was read at Joe's Pub in the Public Theater and directed by
Alex Lippard. His new work, *Amouse Bouche: to please the mouth*, will
hopefully be in workshop when this anthology is released. This is his
first published work.

A dark stage. A lone spotlight follows as **DAVID** *enters from stage right.* **DAVID** *speaks to the audience quickly and directly from memory. He knows these obituaries by heart.*

John Athos. Liked the finer things. John Athos wasn't one to keep his opinions to himself. A bit of a curmudgeon when things didn't go his way, he nonetheless had great love for his many friends. "John was a guy who knew what the best was, and didn't settle for anything less," said roommate William Wells, "I'll miss him terribly, we all will." Born to a prominent Baltimore family he moved to New York seven years ago to pursue acting. Faced with the frustrations of that profession he tried his hand at producing for the theater. The highlight of his producing career came when "Quilted Dreams" opened at the Fourth Street playhouse, a drama about a vibrant young gay man who contracts the AIDS virus. Writing in this paper, our drama critic Louis Addison wrote, "A searing emotional drama, relevant and gripping." When John took a group of friends to his Southampton home, he told them he had the virus, they all cried, at least until John brought out the Chopin vodka. "The only thing that changed in John when he became sick was that he enjoyed life even more, and we didn't think that was possible, but he taught us that, and that's a pretty good legacy," said Mr. Wells. John would surely agree. [*Cell phone begins chirping.*]

Jez Bosala. He had the look. When Jez Bosala left Pittsburgh for New York, he knew New York was the place for him, an accomplished artist and musician with dreams too big for that River city to satisfy. A painting and graphic design student at the Art Academy of Pittsburgh, there he formed a rock group with three other students and all decided to move to New York. Once they arrived each found their own way and the band dissolved. 'Jez loved playing the drums, art, fashion, films, anything creative. He couldn't stand the status quo, he was always trying to push boundaries,' said Virginia Bosala, his mother. Jez had drawn the attention of modeling agencies, and those on the streets of his East Village home, for his unique "London in the 60's" look featuring ascots and multiple belts. Jez had been socializing with friends at a bar and on his way home when he was shot and killed near his Avenue B apartment.

Sally Zane. Only woman in the kitchen. Sally Zane has always been tough. She started as a line cook in a Staten Island diner when she was seventeen and worked her way up to Pastry Chef at Windows on the World by twenty-five. Michael Daniels, executive chef at Windows said, "You have to be tough to work behind the line at any restaurant, especially if you are a pretty young woman like Sally. She took it all, and dished it out pretty good. She was going to be a great chef." Sally missed her high school prom because she had an interview the next day at Manhattan's famed Palinda restaurant. She got the job, and found herself as the only woman in the kitchen, again. A lover of blues and jazz music Sally attended the New Orleans Jazz and Heritage Festival each of the last three years. Her mother, Claire Zane said, "She loved going to New Orleans as much for the music as the great food. Sally was a great kid who I very much admired. I wanted to be like her when I grow up." She was at work at 7 AM on the morning of September 11th. [Cell phone stops.]

I met Sally outside the Maple Leaf Bar. 5'9", blonde hair and wiry with scars all over her arms. We hit if off instantly. She told me she was there from New York, celebrating with friends, going to see funk bands and eating every kind of jambalaya she could find. Me and Sally spent the rest of that night drinking and shaking our ass to the ReBirth Brass Band. She met my friends, my friends met her friends, we all hung out and had a great time. She and I snuck away to a nearby patio, looked at the stars, smoked pot and kissed. I tried to take her back to her hotel but she wouldn't go. We kissed until the sun came up. Later we found a cab and I asked for her number. At the time it didn't make much sense. I could have just left her number in New Orleans but after she looked at me with those grayish, green eyes that said, "You better call me. You won't be disappointed." I flew back to L.A. fixated on Sally's number in my back pocket.

The day after I got back home I called her. I left a message. Five days passed before she called me back and by that last day I was upset. Was it just a vacation fling? Had she been so stoned she wasn't feeling what I felt? Did she have a boyfriend in New York? One morning, the phone rang, I knew it was her. All those doubts vanished. Talking to her made me feel like I was fourteen and just kissed Stephanie Wendell for the first time. We talked about everything: her dreams of opening a restaurant, her promiscuous roommate, and Chet Baker's "Let's Get Lost," her favorite song. Three hours later we managed to hang up. We spoke every day. We argued about which was a better city, New York or L.A. trying to convince the other to move. I usually lost. I called my Mom, told her about Sally, and asked if I could borrow money to fly to New York. She let me use her credit card to book the flight.

As soon as I told Sally I was coming to see her, the conversations changed. She told me all the naughty things she was going to do to me. I never performed phone sex before, but she was so into it I forced myself to catch on. She had elaborate fantasies involving sex in cabs, restaurant bathrooms, elevators in strange buildings, in bedrooms at parties. I had only kissed this girl, okay, we kissed for three hours, but she felt free enough to express her dark fantasies. The conversations pushed the boundaries of flexibility, endurance and legality. You definitely do not forget the first time only the sound of another persons voice makes you come.

I'm picturing you in a silk robe. That's nice. [And what are you wearing?] My fuzzy green robe of course. [Of course, silly me. Tell me what else I can do?] Sit down in the chair. [On you?] No, just in the chair. [Am I naked?] Yes. [Am I tied up?] Yes. [Blindfolded?] Yes. [And then what?] I kiss your lips, while touching your breasts, I slowly move down to your neck. [Are you playing with my nipples?] Yes, I kiss your nipples, lightly biting them, I kiss your stomach, run my tongue, along your stomach, I spread your legs, I kiss your inner thighs, I lift your legs and kiss you on the back of your thighs, you are moaning, you beg me to put my tongue inside you. [And do you?] Not yet, I kiss your lips, I pull your hair. [And softly bite me?] Yes, I put my fingers in your mouth. [And I suck them hard and deep . . . just like I sucked you.] And then I slowly pull them out, I am not touching you anywhere, I am looking at you. [And I beg you to put it in me.] Bound at the wrists, blindfolded, moaning squirming I put my tongue inside you. Your moaning gets louder you taste so good. [And you touch me lightly.] My tongue is so deep inside you. [I want it deeper, deeper, and you tease me with your touch.] I take off the cuffs, and lay you down on the floor. [Still blindfolded?] Yes, and I put my cock in your mouth, and my tongue inside you. [And I grab your ass and pull you deeper.] Yes, God, Sally you have me so hard, I want to fuck you so badly. [Too bad you aren't here.] I know. [Why don't you touch yourself?] Oh I am. [Right now?] The whole time. [Are you going to come?] Yes.

You also don't forget hearing your first rape fantasy in which you are cast as the aggressor. Or in telling your first as the victim.

When we weren't on the phone, I taught myself and my students how to play, "Let's get lost." We corresponded via email, and those became filled with sex too. I never checked my email as much as when this was going on. We talked about regular stuff too. I learned about her parents, her Father, Jack, a Jaguar mechanic, remarried in Scottsdale, Arizona, and her Mother, Claire, a real estate agent as well as an active member of the Staten Island Historical Society.

New York was less than two weeks away. I rearranged my teaching schedule, and Sally requested a few days off from Windows. Everything was set. In the last few weeks I had gotten really good at playing "Let's

Get Lost." I decided I would record it for my next CD, my New York CD. The night before I left, a friend, Ralph, from the Knauss Gallery in Santa Monica called to see if I could play at his gallery opening. It would be an extra fifty bucks in my pocket and it was a good omen. The gig lasted four hours and I played her song three times. The SuperShuttle honked at 5:45 AM the next morning and I was on my way . . . to Sally. During the flight, Pennsylvania and New Jersey sped beneath me, and there she was, in a little denim skirt and tank top. I wanted to rip her clothes off right there in the terminal. Hers were the wettest kisses of my life. We kissed and groped the whole cab ride in, Mohammed al-Mohammed didn't seem to mind. Neither did Elmo from Sesame Street though our seatbelts definitely weren't fastened. We were in her bed pressing our bodies together. No whips, no hand-cuffs, no oils, no hood of the car in midtown traffic, just great hot-in-the-bedroom-both-hitting-orgasms-sweating-in-the-busted-air-conditioned-apartment-avoid-the-wet-spot-later sex. I was giddy, and then I took a nap. She woke me up with kisses, telling me to take a shower and get dressed, we had nine o'clock reservations.

That was the beginning of a weeklong parade of food, sex, partying, music, and revelry of life in the summer in Manhattan. One night she cooked for me. Salmon gravlox, sautéed zucchini and squash, a bottle of Opus One. After a chocolate soufflé for dessert, I played "Let's Get Lost." We didn't make it out of the kitchen until the sun came through the windows. I decided on the plane that I was going to move to New York. I told her on the air-phone.

She said "It's the sex talking, wait a week." "It's not just the sex, and it's not talking, it's screaming at me through a bullhorn from five feet away." When I thought about who or what I'd miss from L.A., all I could come up with was two students and a few record company contacts. And KLON my favorite Jazz radio station. And the Playboy Jazz Festival at the Hollywood Bowl every June. That was a great party, one of the few times all of L.A, black, white, Latin, Asian, get together to have a good time and listen to music. But that was it: Two kids, one two-day party, and a radio station. New York had Sally and her friends and the city and Sally.

When I got home, I called my Mom. She told me if that was what I wanted to do, she'd support me. I asked Sally if she would put me up if I moved there. She said wait, she missed me, but it was too soon after I returned. The next night, I wrote her a long email, telling her "How thoroughly I've gone over the scenario and this is what I want." New York was what I wanted. Sally was who I wanted. And Birdland, the Village Vanguard, the Blue Note, Iridium, those were the clubs I wanted to play.

We were reasonable. It's just a fling. It will pass. It didn't. I said goodbye to my friends. I recommended other teachers for my guitar students. I sold my car to an old drummer, I called my landlord to give up the apartment, I cancelled the phone, turned off the cable, the power, the gas, the *L.A. Times*. I changed the address on my student loan, and *Down Beat* subscription to Sally's apartment; I called my cell phone company and got a New York number. It happened seemingly overnight. I was practicing my guitar one night. I played everything faster. "'Round Midnight," a tune I'd always played slowly, sounded like fiery be-bop. I didn't know what was happening to me. Everything in my life had sped up. My life, my pulse, even my music. Everything was faster. After one week in New York and making the decision to move there, the speed was in my blood. The pace of my life in L.A. had accelerated to the pace of my week in New York, and I had to get back. I needed the speed, I needed Sally. How did this happen?

I was in New York; Sally was at work when my plane landed. I rode to her Chinatown apartment. Her roommate, Jessica, let me in. I dropped off my stuff and walked down to her restaurant, Windows on the

World. I bought roses from a deli, and rode the elevator ninety-eight floors up, my ears popping. The Maitre d' smiled and said, "David, right?" That made me smile. I walked past a window and gasped. The Empire State Building, Central Park, I could see the Atlantic Ocean, a perfect day. He showed me to the kitchen.

She screamed when she saw me and ran out from behind the line and gave me a big hug and a wet kiss. She took the flowers, put them in a vase and the Maitre d' put them on the host stand. He offered to buy me a drink, but since Sally had to go back to work, I declined, but I did mention that was available if they needed a solo jazz guitar player for the restaurant. He told me he'd check with the G.M. I blew Sally a kiss and walked to the elevator. I went back to her apartment. When I arrived Jessica was walking a guy covered in tattoos to the door, I said hello, and went into Sally's room.

Jez Bosala. . . . Dreams too big for that River city to satisfy . . . drums, art, fashion, films, anything creative . . . couldn't stand the status quo . . . shot and killed near his Avenue B apartment.

I opened a copy of the *Village Voice* and began looking for Jazz clubs. I called up a few, spoke to their bookers and prepared to mail out my CD. Sally called me and told me about a free jazz show in Central Park that afternoon. I packed my guitar, a box of CDs, and boarded the subway. I passed a man with half of his head shaved sitting in the subway playing Beatles covers, and I thought, "I can do that, but do I want to? Is that how I want to make money today? The average subway rider is probably more likely to drop a quarter in the guitar case of a man playing "Yesterday" than Miles Davis's "So What." I arrived in Central Park and couldn't believe I was still in New York City. I loved the Ramble. Aside from a few gay men on the cruise, it was so beautiful and lush. Birds chirping. Squirrels hunting for nuts.

I was back in Ohio getting stoned in the woods cutting a Music Theory class.

A muscular and deeply tan man wearing a wife beater said, "Hello," and asked my name. I said, David, and walked away. He asked where I was going, and I told him to make some money. He said he would pay me if I wanted. I sped up out of the Ramble.

I found the free show. I listened to the quartet play for a few songs, and then I looked for an area to set up my own stage: a large Oak tree with low overhanging branches providing good acoustics. I ran through some standards, crowd pleasers, the jazz equivalent of Beatles covers. People walked past and tossed change in my guitar case, one older balding guy stood, nodding to three songs, bought my CD, and told me his name was Louis. While I was chatting with Louis another man appeared. He was dressed in blue corduroys wearing two belts across his pelvis and butt, neither hooked into the belt loops, a white oxford shirt with a blue striped tie, tied under his shirt like an ascot, and long dark hair to his collar covering most of his face. He was studying me like an art critic studying a painting he doesn't quite understand. Louis left and this guy kept staring. Something inside me said, "Impress this guy" so I played an obscure and complicated Mingus tune. I messed up the bridge but otherwise played decently. In the middle of the song he asked me "Where'd you get your T-shirt?" "L.A." He introduced himself as Jez and said "You're cool." He took one of my CDs and told me he'd call me. Before I could ask him for the money he was gone. I played another hour and quit. I sold three CDs, and made eight bucks in loose change for a grand total of thirty-eight dollars. I headed to the subway back to Sally.

I opened a beer and my phone rang. It was Sally, she told me to take off all my clothes climb into bed and keep my eyes closed. I laughed and obeyed her. A few minutes later I heard her enter the apartment and come into the bedroom. She pulled the sheet off me and began kissing my chest and removing her clothes. Soon sweat was mingling, fingernails pressed into flesh, tongues lips saliva everywhere. I took a nap.

An hour later, my phone rang; it was Jez. Could I play a gig with him that night. He was a drummer and needed a guitar player, a duo, him and I, at a club called Morrie's on the Lower East Side, fifty bucks for two sets. I said yes, and Sally became very excited. We arrived and drank a beer while waiting. There was a small drum kit already set up on stage. On the wall: Monk, Miles, Coltrane, the same posters I had in my teenage bedroom. Jez arrived and said, "Play the same stuff you played in the park." I plugged my guitar into the small crappy house amp and did a brief sound check. There were about ten people in the bar. Sally was the only one paying attention. She blew me a kiss and I began playing "Let's Get Lost." Jez followed me perfectly, I signaled for the change but he had his eyes closed. He hit it right on the beat. During "Mood Indigo," Jez asked if I could buy any brand of shoes right now, what would they be and why. I laughed and told him Campers, because they were comfortable and stylish. He nodded and said "We'll do 'Round Midnight' next, but play it fast." My playing became more relaxed and we got a nice round of applause from the twenty-five people in the room. I looked out at Sally and saw her wipe away a tear.

As Jez and I packed up our gear, I looked over at him and asked, "What kind of shoes would you buy?" He said, "Billy Martin snakeskin cowboy boots with a low heel. I have them on layaway." We were all sitting at a table when Morrie came over, paid us, bought us a round of shots, and Jez lit up a joint. "Eight more payments and they are mine."

Jez passed the joint to Sally who took a hit and said, "This guy Carmine, from Tottenville, we'd drive around in his Cutlass while he sold bags of weed. He'd always run out of baggies. Carmine knew every grocery store on Staten Island and exactly which aisle they kept the plastic sandwich bags. The selection was usually amazing. Think about it. How often do you buy sandwich bags? Once every three months?" "Never," Jez and I agreed. "And yet, the shelves are filled with different brands of plastic baggies. Why is that? The plastic sandwich bag manufacturers know that pot dealers are important and valued customers, and yet there is no way on God's green Earth they can directly market to the dealers so they have to be subtle. Look at the colors of the boxes. Glad is yellow and green, Baggies, red and yellow, Ziplocs, green and red. *All the colors of the Rastafarian flag*, something every single pot smoker in the world can identify. When you go to Amsterdam and want to find a coffee shop that sells pot, you look for the green, red, and yellow Rasta flag in the window. That's how you know. Same with the plastic bags aisle. Do you think some housewife in Kansas is going to make that connection?"

Jez looked over at me, took a hit, and said, "Your girlfriend is a genius, hold on to her."

In bed she said this was a special occasion, she introduced me to something special, a "Personal Lubricant," called Astroglide. Sally rubbed it on me and it felt like . . . It was as if . . . You know how good K-Y Jelly feels? Astroglide is about fifty times better. I have never felt anything that great in life, ever.

I woke up in the middle of the night to use the bathroom. I ran into a strange naked man with a ponytail coming out of Jessica's room.

Who are you? [Who are you?] I live here, I'm Sally's boyfriend. [I'm here right now. I just got done fucking Jessica. Who's Sally?] Her roommate. I guess you didn't get that far. [I got as far as I needed to.]

Not only was he naked but his penis was still full and erect. He had literally just finished. He noticed me noticing him and said, "You want some too?" I walked into Sally's room. I had a difficult time falling asleep. Especially when Jessica and Mr. Pony Tail began Round Two. I was annoyed but fascinated by their grunting and moaning. It sounded like he knew I was awake and demanding I listen. Maybe Sally and I had been too loud and this was payback. Ponytail practically screamed, "God I love fucking you." And that was it. Silence. Once they finished, I fell asleep. At 6 AM the next morning Sally got up to work the breakfast shift, and I woke up with her. I told her the story of Jessica and Pony Tail man.

[I told you she was a slut. I don't care. It's her life.] Do you know this guy? [I think his name is Todd.] And you don't care? [You need to look for your own place.] [*Beat.*] What? [I'm not throwing you out, but you need to start looking.] I just had my first gig, and now this? [I'm falling in love with you but I don't want to resent you being here. It's starting and I hate that. We are not ready to live together and you know that.] I'll start looking today.

She kissed me and went to work. I went back to sleep. I woke up a few hours later to the sound of my cell phone ringing. It was my Mom.

[Are you okay?] Yeah, I'm fine Mom. What's wrong? [We're being attacked. Turn on the TV.]

I got up and turned on the TV. I stared. I walked to the fire escape and saw a big cloud of black smoke and 1,000 people on the usually empty Manhattan Bridge, all staring at the Cloud. Jessica came outside.

[Please tell me she's still in bed.] No. She had to work breakfast.

Jessica started bawling. I walked back into Sally's room and put on pants, a long sleeve T-shirt, a baseball hat, running shoes, and my glasses. I had to go find her. I walked down to the street. As soon as I was in the street walking towards the black Cloud I overheard, "They hit the White House too. What's next?" People were streaming past me away from the Cloud, covered in soot, disheveled and crying. A topless man held his shirt over an elderly woman's face so she could breathe. Near a statue of Confucius, a hospital worker handed me a surgical mask. I took one, thinking, I won't need it. Behind the Federal Court house a US Marshal held a shotgun and pointed it at anyone who approached. I walked closer to the Cloud. I didn't know the streets down there. I neared the Cloud. I had to find her. The surgical mask on my face was the only reason I could continue. I entered the Cloud.

Inches of ash and dust covered my shoes like fresh snowfall, and the only sound was my feet on the ash. Scraps of charred paper burned on the ground. Total silence. In the Cloud, a silent car drove past emitting a dim light from its headlamps.

As I walked along a building a photographer said to me, "This building's warm, it's gonna go next." We walked away from the building. I passed a row of burned out cars and thought of Beirut and Northern Ireland. I arrived at the site: a two-story remainder of rubble that was the World Trade Center, and Windows on the World. I approached a fireman standing by his totaled fire truck.

My girlfriend was in there. Where do I go? He looked at me and said, "My Company's in there. I overslept." A fireman called out, "Joey" and the man walked away from me.

Church bells began ringing. How poignant. I looked at my watch, 12 Noon. It wasn't poignant at all. Something still worked down there: The church bells. Walking around in the rubble I saw a pink Chanel shoe, a pair of tortoise shell glasses, a fax machine, a defibrillator. Sally wasn't there. No one was there but firemen and cops.

Maybe she got out in time and went home. I walked towards Broadway and saw a bank of telephones. I picked one up and heard the dial tone. A sweet sound. I dialed Sally's number. [*Ringing. Ringing.*]

[Hi . . .] My heart stopped. [. . . it's Sally. Please leave a message.]

I called Jessica.

[Hello?] It's David. [Oh.] Did she call yet? [No. Where are you?] I'm down here in the rubble. [Get outta there, they're gonna attack again!]

She hung up the phone.

I walked up Broadway, past an overturned cart. Bagels and Snapples everywhere. The sun was emerging through the Cloud. I was at Broadway and Canal. I began sobbing. Uncontrollable. I rested my head on my arm on a trashcan. Then I fell to the street crying. I felt someone's arms around my chest and a head resting on my back—comforting me as tears fell. After five minutes of this I slowly stopped crying. The arms released me. I wiped the snot and tears away and turned to thank the arms that held me but they were gone. I looked up and down the street but it could have been anyone, or no one.

I began my walk back to Sally's. The sun was high, bright and warm. I saw a cocker spaniel take a dump in the street and its owner clean the poop. The world was as close as it's ever come to ending and this woman curbs her dog.

Jessica ran to the door when I opened it, disappointed to see me. I removed my clothes so drenched in gray soot they created a small ash cloud. I took my cell phone into the bathroom and checked my messages. On the TV: planes flying into the World Trade Center, people jumping from the Towers, people in some unnamed Arab country celebrating. Off. I went into Sally's room and noticed her bra on the floor and I cried. I walked to the fire escape to watch the police cars, ambulances, perimeters being erected. My phone rang. I jumped. It was Jez.

[Are you okay?] Sally was at work. [Where?] Windows on the World. [Fuck. Have you heard from her?] No. [We're at Morrie's if you want to get a drink.] She might call. [Bring your cell phone.] Right, thanks. I think I'll do that.

When I saw Jez we hugged. I barely knew him but he was my best friend in New York. We chain-drank bourbon and talked: How I came to New York, his childhood in Pittsburgh, movies, everything but what just happened. My eyes burned. I asked around for eye drops but no one had any. I told Jez I needed to find some and he agreed to walk with me. Finding eye drops in Manhattan is not hard. September 11th, it took two hours. When I finally found the drops they felt as good on my scarred red eyes as the Astroglide still coated to my stomach. Jez and I walked back to Sally's. No one. I left a note for Sally to please call me on my cell phone. We sat around the living room watching the news but didn't have much to say. I walked into her room and cried. Jez asked me about a tune from last night, "Play it for me." I played the song but it was lousy.

We went back to Morrie's. Once we returned to the bar it was filled with very drunk people not paying attention to CNN. Jez and I continued drinking bourbon. My cell phone rang, I jumped, it was Jessica. She told me to call Sally's Mom, Claire, on Staten Island. I debated it.

[Hello.] Hi, it's David, Sally's boyfriend. [Have you heard from her?] No. Have you? [No. When did you see her last?] This morning, when she left for work. [She definitely went?] She left the apartment. I don't know that she went there, but where else would she have gone at 7 AM? [Nowhere.] [*Beat.*] [I'm afraid to leave the house. I don't want to miss her call.] I understand. [We should meet.] Yes. Soon. [Please call me anytime.] You too. [Take care of yourself.] I will. [Okay.] Good-bye. [Good-bye.] I ordered another bourbon. This was a rare occasion where no matter how much I drank, I did not get drunk. I should have been wrecked by now, but Jez and I just sat there, not really talking, just drinking.

The days bled into each other. The bourbon flowed, sometimes Jez and I drank beer just for variety but the objective was the same. No sign of Sally. Everyday I read the *Times* "Portraits of Grief," listened to the radio, watched the news and cried. I walked around to watch the people, dazed. I'd ride the subway going nowhere, just to ride, and people were ghosts, not looking at each other, not talking to each other, quiet, deferring to strangers, numbed.

Then the flags flew and the slogans emerged. "We Will Not Let Them Destroy Our Spirit." "I Love New York More Than Ever." "Osama bin Laden, Wanted Dead or Alive."

Morrie held a "Come As Your Favorite Patriot" costume party, with an open bar. I borrowed a black curly wig from Jez, and found a headband in Sally's underwear drawer. I put on a tie-dye T-shirt and went as Carlos Santana. Jez wore the same clothes he always wore. We danced. We played quarters. I drank a shot of tequila from the large breasts of a woman dressed as a cross between Betsy Ross and Courtney Love. A bartender handed me my cell phone. I had a message. It was Claire. They called. Sally was confirmed dead. I only walked half a block when my knees buckled and I fell to the ground. Laying on Ludlow Street beating my arms into the concrete. Today no stranger's arms comforted me. I stood up, wiped the snot away, and walked home. Back to Sally's. I walked in and saw Jessica. She knew. I went into Sally's room, slammed the door, and lay in her bed. Jessica came in and sat on the bed crying. She lay down next to me. We held each other. She told me she returning home to Dallas and never coming back.

I called my Mom.

[Come home.] I can't. [Why not?] I can't leave New York. Sally brought me here, and I owe it to her to stay. [You know if you change your mind you can always come home.] I know Mom. [I love you.] I love you, too. I have to go back to the bar to close my tab.

She laughed.

Back at Morrie's Jez drank. My bourbon was still there, all water. I finished it in one swig.

[Do you like comic books?] I read Silver Surfer when I was eight. [Morrie's hired us for a weekly gig. We start next week.] I have no idea what day it is, how could I know when next week starts?

And that's how the next days went. I drank with Jez, slept on the couch, watched the news, cried over the paper, managed to eat a can of Spaghetti O's once a day and that was my life in New York without Sally. Rumors of another attack spread. The day our weekly residency began I was drinking up until the minute we walked on stage, and I had a drink there too. I played horribly. Jez played horribly. The crowd of about fifty people applauded after each number. Morrie took pity on us. He should have fired us; instead he kept buying us drinks. I was vomiting in the morning, the apartment was a mess, I'd go days without a shower or eating. Anthrax started showing up in letters. And released in the subway, people said. Everyone was terrified of white powder. Jez asked if I liked Phillip K. Dick.

No, I don't like Phillip K. Dick. Why don't you take your stupid fucking questions and shove them up your ass!

John Athos. Liked the finer things . . . great love for his many friends . . . didn't settle for anything less . . . Quilted Dreams . . . the AIDS virus . . . John brought out the Chopin vodka . . . he enjoyed life even more.

My mom called asking if I'd purchased my ticket to Ron and Trina's wedding in Rome. Bourbon and misery made me forget that my friend from high school was getting married in two weeks in Rome. Mom said she'd buy my plane ticket for me. I still owed her money for the ticket to see Sally and now she was buying me another one? I had to go. I had to get away, out of New York. Out of America. But to get on an airplane? In October? Weeks after this madness? I needed to. To see some beauty. To see <u>something created</u>. To stop drinking for at least one day. To go to Rome, somewhere that understands this level of suffering.

I ride the Staten Island ferry across the Harbor. The Cloud remains where the site used to stand. Minutes later the Statue of Liberty looms over us. [*Silence.*]

A cab takes me to Tottenville. To her house. I ring the bell. A woman, petite with white hair, still in her bathrobe, still devastated, comes to the door. It's Claire.

[Yes?] I'm David. I am Sally's . . . I was Sally's . . . We spoke, before . . . [Yes.] Unsure what to do, she embraces me. [Come in.]

I enter what must have once been a lovely antique-filled home. Now, it's been wrecked by weeks of neglect: newspapers everywhere, half-finished coffee mugs, a small brown cat licks a plate of spaghetti on the living room floor.

[Can I get you anything?] Oh, no. I'm fine. [*Beat.*] I mean, I'm not fine . . . I'm . . . [I'm glad you came.] How are you? [How is a woman's who's outlived her daughter supposed to be?] I have no idea. [I don't either. Look at my house.] It looks like my house . . . Sally's house . . . Where I'm staying now. [Do you know anyone else who died?] I'm sorry? [In the attacks? Was Sally the only one?] Yeah. [I wonder how others are coping.] I'm sure there's a group or something. A number you can call. [What is it?] Sorry? [The number. To call the coping group?] I don't know what it is; I just assume there must be one. [Oh.] [*Beat.*] I could find it for you. [Would you?] Sure. [*Beat.*] [Now.] Oh. Sure. Are any of these newspapers current? [I don't know. I was looking for information about Sally.]

I pick up a page of the *Daily News*.

Do you know where the telephone is? [On the wall in the kitchen.]

I go into the kitchen and find a cordless phone. I dial a number. [*Beat.*] Push a button. Listen. Then another button. Still listening. And another. [*Beat.*] We're on hold. [I see.] Hello? Yes, I'd like some information about any World Trade Center survivor's groups . . . In Staten Island . . . Okay. Do you have a pen?

Claire slowly looks around the room. [*In the kitchen.*] I stare at her for a moment, then go to the kitchen to find a pen. I write the number on a piece of paper.

Thank you.

I dial the number.

[Thank you.] You're welcome. I'm calling about the survivor's group. [*Beat.*] Oh, good. Uh, when and where is the next meeting? [*Beat.*] Okay, great. Thank you.

I hand her the piece of paper. Without looking at it, she sets it atop of a pile of newspapers next to her.

There's a meeting at 8 PM tonight at 4573 Arthur Kill Road. Do you know where that is? [Yes.] So you'll go? [Yes. Thank you.] You're welcome. [Come with me.] [*Beat.*] [Tonight.] I, uh can't . . . I have a gig . . . I play music . . . I'm, a musician. [I see.] But you should go. [Sally told me you were a musician.] Yeah. [*Beat.*] [I miss her so much.]

Mom tells me to be safe. How exactly can we be safe? Sally was at work. Cooking food in a restaurant like she's done every day of her adult life. Nothing is safe. Columnists write that this was a long time in the works, only a matter of time, American Imperialism's comeuppance. Was <u>Sally</u> responsible for that? Her Nike's were made in Taiwanese sweatshops, her Calvin Klein bra in Hong Kong, her Diesel skirt by Croatian children, she <u>died</u> for that? No. I'm going to Rome.

I'm not letting fucking murdering terrorists tell me I can't go see my friend get married.

I apologized to Jez, but he had some issues about my trip: [What if the plane gets hijacked?] [What if they hit the Vatican when you're there?] [Rome is filled with landmarks.] [You'll be more easily identified as an American there.] [With everything that's happened, why risk it?] [Now is not the time to poke the terrorists in the eye with a stick.]

The truth is, I'm terrified to fly. For the first time in my life. But I'm not letting terrorists tell me I can't. As I fill my luggage, I'm asking myself, does this make me look like an American? The shoes: Red Pumas or Grey New Balance? Puma is a German company but the shoes are bright red, too flashy, they scream tourist. New Balance is an American company, does bin Laden know this?

I am convinced I am going to Rome to die.

I left for JFK five hours before my flight. Check-in took ten minutes. As I got through the metal detectors *a seventeen-year-old boy* stood in full battle fatigues holding a semi-automatic rifle. This was supposed to be reassuring? My bags are searched four times. I sat, reading the *New York Times*. Security is important, but if the Marines thought me and my bags are secure, some putz who couldn't get a job driving a cab going through my luggage a fifth time isn't going to reassure me of anything. I finally boarded the plane.

The plane was half full of Wisconsin Catholics making their suddenly discounted pilgrimage to Rome. They were uniformly obese and wore T-shirts declaring, "I'm with stupid" and professing their allegiance to Coors Light Beer. This plane is going down. There's no doubt now. The al-Qaeda benchwarmers are going to take it out just for target practice.

I slept away the flight and was groggy when I awoke in Rome that morning. One full day without booze and I felt horrible, jet-lagged and dehydrated. The long commute into the city in a comfy Mercedes micro-bus was piloted by Giovanni at 145 kilometers per hour.

The Colloseum appeared in the distance towering over Rome and I became excited. I arrived in my hotel near the Spanish Steps. In the room was a note from Ron and Trina inviting me to lunch with them at Vigo's café down the street. I noticed the tiny beds and took a shower. Walking among the Romans, it was nice to be somewhere that wasn't full of grief. I noticed this immediately.

At lunch I met John.

Charmed, he said when he met me.

John was a funny bitter hypochondriac, always complaining, and smoking, a former theater producer with one financially successful play in a ten-year career. Now he was sick and lived with Bill. After lunch everyone went their separate ways but John and I stayed in the café, drinking, watching the Roman's pass. A fat man wore a T-shirt saying, "I'm With Stupid." The kids rode scooters and Vespas, screaming through the streets much too fast. "I'm With Stupid" saw me and waved.

After six hours of drinking, I told John I had a headache and he handed me a pill that I took immediately. We had one more drink together, things became hazy and then he put two more pills in my hand and told me to take them when I woke up. I walked across the street to the hotel where I stumbled up the stairs to my room. I drifted away to sleepy-sleepyland, my contacts still in my eyes, my shoes on my feet, two pills in my hand. I awoke to darkness outside the window. I looked at my watch. 2:23 AM. I took one of the pills and fell back asleep. Morning came and I awoke, strangely refreshed.

Down at Vigo's John read an Italian newspaper, "Anthrax letters sent to Tom Brokaw." I took the second pill. "Good man." He ordered me a cup of coffee in what sounded like perfect Italian. As I sat there, drinking my coffee, I realized I hadn't thought about Sally in two days. I was asleep on a plane for one, and comatose for the second, but still.

John and I walked to the Pantheon. I told John about the fight Sally and I had the morning she died. I began to cry, surrounded by tourists, talking to a man I'd known six hours. He hugged me and it was such a warm feeling, I cried harder. John told me he was HIV-positive. I immediately stopped. I didn't know what to say. I said, I'm sorry. I noticed his eyes had a defeated wisdom to them. We hugged a little while longer and I realized that now I was comforting him. I leaned in and kissed his cheek.

His eyes no longer looked defeated and wise, they look surprised and hopeful. We ended the hug and he said, "Let's get out of here before we get bashed." We discovered a fountain a few blocks away. Tourists milled around us as we stared at the water, he put his hand on my back. It felt comfortable; he leaned in and kissed me on the cheek.

Listen . . . [This is where you tell me you're not gay, right?] I'm not. [I'm too old to play these games anymore. When I was twenty-five it was fun. Now, I'm over it.]

He walked away. I went after him.

John, wait. [Oh, how romantic you followed me. Why?]

He was hurt. He turned and continued his walk. I let him go. I went back to the Fountain. What was happening? I hug a man in Rome, I kiss him, he kisses me and now I have to figure out if I'm gay.

I am attracted to John. That's the bottom line. I want to be sexual with him. He is HIV-positive. I don't care.

I walk back to the hotel. He was not at Vigo's where we met. I found out his room number and I knocked on the door. No reply. I went off to the Spanish Steps. John sat smoking a cigarette.

Hey. [Hey.] I want to kiss you. [Don't fuck with me.] I do. [I thought you weren't gay.] I don't know what I am. I know I'm attracted to you. [Why?] I don't know. You're attractive, so I'm attracted to you.

I pushed his hand away, knocking the lit cigarette to the ground and kissed him on the mouth, deep and French. It was a strange wonderful experience. Stubble, mixed with his tongue pressing hot warm saliva and the stench of tobacco around in my mouth. I stopped and looked at him. He smiled.

[Kissing boys, eh? What would Sally say?] I stared at him in disbelief. I turned and walked away and he followed. [I'm sorry, it was a joke. I thought you'd never talk to me again, much less kiss me.] I stopped walking. Don't mention Sally to me ever again. I walked away. [Fine.I won't. I'm sorry. We'll talk later.] I continued walking back to the hotel.

At the rehearsal dinner in a restaurant called Beatrice's, Ron and Trina greeted people at the door. They gave me what I now recognize as the "I didn't know you were gay" look. They saved a seat next to John for me. I considered telling them I'm not gay, and I'd be happier sitting with Ron's parents, but I don't. The dining room was in the basement and decorated with black and white photos of famous Roman's who ate at Beatrice's. John was talking to his roommate Bill when I arrived. He glanced at me, smiled, and said hello. There were two empty seats across from me. A waiter filled my wine glass and I drank a sip. A moment later Trina sat two gorgeous women across from me. Brandy, the blonde, was an account exec at an ad agency in Manhattan, and Kierstan, with dark hair, did PR for Donna Karan. They talked about their jobs, their gyms, their manicures, shopping in Rome, restaurants they're dying to go to, chefs who are so over, clubs they love, clubs they hate, all the while, John had his hand on my knee, and I pushed it off, and he put it back, and I pushed it off again. Trina came over during the second course and told Brandy I was an amazing guitar player, and they should all get together the next time I have a gig. Kierstan asked where I play in New York and when I say Morrie's, neither have heard of it. John leans in and says, "It's a dump on the Lower East Side and the only place in the city that would allow David to play there. Right, honey." The girls laughed and John smiled and put his hand on mine on top of the table. I playfully patted his hand and removed mine. John leaned in and whispered, "He's shy. Isn't it adorable." The girls laughed. Brandy asked, "So you guys are dating?" "No!" John, looking horrified stood up and yelled, "I will not let you assfuck me in the morning and then deny it later that night!" The room went silent. "You can get away with that with those little Chelsea whores but not me!" He threw his napkin on the table, knocked over a chair, and walked out of the restaurant. The girls cuddled together, covering their mouths to keep from laughing. I looked at them and I heard myself say, "I don't know what he's talking about, I'm not even gay." I followed after him.

I didn't have to go very far. Out on the street he is doubled over laughing through tears. What the hell is your problem?

[Oh my God, that was the greatest.] What the fuck, John? [The look on your face. I'll remember it forever.] Great. [All I wanted to do was hold your hand. And you kept pushing it away. So that's what you get.] That's what I get? I came here to relax to get away from New York. [You came here for the same reason everyone goes to weddings and vacations: to get laid.] Do you remember me telling you about a girl named Sally who I was in love with? She died in the World Trade Center? [I remember Sally; I also saw Brandy and Kierstan. Which one did you want? The blonde? The brunette? Both? How about all three of us? Don't tell me it hasn't crossed your mind. I've got some Ecstasy; I'll put it in their drinks. We'll take a pill and see if we can get them into bed. That'll be how I'll make it up to you. Deal?] I've known Ron since I was fourteen. His parents are friends with my Mom. [Looks like you better call Mom. My advice would be to just speak from the heart. I have a hunch she'll understand.] I'm not gay! Keep shouting. Maybe you'll convince the doves.]

I turned away from John and walked down the block. Holy Christ. I came here to get away, and now this? Ron came jogging down the street toward me.

[David, wait up.] Go back inside, enjoy yourself. [What was that?] I told him about Sally, he told me about AIDS. We had a connection. I kissed him. He wanted to hold my hand under the table and I wouldn't let him. That was his revenge. [He pulls this stuff all the time. He loves attention. No one really believes what he says. At least not Bill or Trina or me, or anyone who knows him.] What about your parents? [We just told them about John. We told the whole party. He does this to Bill once a week. Come back inside. It'll be fine.] He does this all the time? [It's his thing. What can I say? He keeps things interesting.] I guess so. [You kissed him?]

We walked back into the dining room. When I arrived, people laughed. I sat down and finished my glass of wine. It was quickly refilled. A few minutes later, John returned. He tapped me on the shoulder, I turned around. He had a big smile. I stood up and held out my hand. We shook hands and then I threw the full glass of wine in his face. Everyone cheered and applauded. Not very original, but sweet nonetheless. He laughed, accepting this, and left to change clothes. That chicken Parmesan so crispy and tender. The chocolate tartuffo, rich and smooth.

Everyone went to an Irish bar, the Black Duke, filled with Guinness posters, Oasis and The Who on the stereo, drunk Brits and other Americans. As the wine, and bourbon shots flowed, I told Kierstan how Ron and Trina met at the Grange Hall. We also talked about *Kierstan's love of sushi, Kierstan's love of Jimmy Choo's, Kierstan's sudden appreciation for jazz guitarists.* We were back in my hotel room in 90 seconds. It was drunk and sloppy.

Where are you going? [I'm going to take my tampon out and then we are gonna fuck.]

She pulled my pants down and began sucking. <u>Nothing</u> was happening. I pulled her up and kissed her, but she kept going down on me. I was drunk and she wasn't having success. Eventually she stopped.

Don't I turn you on? [Yes.] Then what's the problem? [I'm pretty drunk, I guess.] You're not gay? [No. If I were, I'd be with John, not you.] Maybe you should be.

She got dressed and left. I passed out with my contacts in, again.

The next morning, the sun broke through the windows and I woke up, head pounding. I looked at the floor and saw a bra. Sally.

I am a man on autopilot. I am not thinking about the consequences of anything I'm doing.

A shower made me feel a little better. Not much. I went to Vigo's for coffee. John was there reading the paper.

Good Morning . . . I said, Good morning. [I thought the angry diva wine in the face routine would be the <u>end</u> of your revenge.] What are you talking about? [You are the king of Denial.] How is anything I do your business? [You kiss me, you fuck Kierstan. Who's next? Trina? Ron, perhaps?] I didn't fuck her. [Too drunk? Poor baby. I have some Viagra, you should have called me.] Why are you being like this? [Because I have a crush on you. I thought our kiss meant something.] It did until you made a clown of me. [Oh get over it. Everyone else has.] I didn't know what I was getting into with you. I guess I thought we could kiss without it meaning that we were <u>married</u>. I told you before I've never kissed a man before. [And I'm telling you, I've been lots of men's first real kiss. And none of them treated me as badly as you have. Drink your coffee and don't talk to me.]

I sat at a table next to John's, drank coffee and read the *International Herald Tribune*. Anthrax sent to Tom Daschle's office in the Senate.

I'm sorry. [No you're not.] No, I am. [Well it does you no good.] Why? [Because I don't forgive you.] Come on. I'm sorry. What do you want from me? [Prove it.] How? [I need a new tie for the wedding. Go shopping with me.] Prada? [It's so much cheaper here than New York.]

We finished our coffee and went to Prada. As we walked in, Kierstan and Brandy walked out. I didn't care.

In a marble chapel near the hotel the wedding ceremony was conducted entirely in Italian. John and I couldn't see the altar blocked by two photographers, an assistant whose shoes squeaked on the marble, and two videographers. We told quiet jokes, and made fun of people's outfits.

The reception in a beautiful palazzo had a cheesy band playing American pop music. I played "Twist and Shout" with the band and everyone applauded. I looked over at John who walked out of the room. I followed him up to my hotel room. He had his hands all over my body, kissing me, arousing me, touching me exactly how I liked to be touched. I thought, "Harder," he did it harder. I thought "To the left," he went left. I thought "Stop," he stopped. It was amazing. He put a condom on and plenty of Astroglide and it felt great. He came, and fell asleep with his arms around me. I fell asleep later.

I awoke the next morning to a note and two white pills, "Bill and I are off to Amsterdam for three days, then back to New York. Call me when we return. Love, John. P.S. Take one pill now, another when the plane takes off." I called Mom.

[*That weird international ring.*] [Hi, it's Sally, leave a message.] Hi, uh . . . I, really miss you . . . I don't know what's going on . . . I met . . .

I hung up the phone and checked my itinerary. My flight left at 5 PM that afternoon, and it was . . . 1 PM. I threw my clothes in my bag, and called down to arrange an airport transfer. I swallowed the pill, and checked under the bed. Nothing. I climbed in the car, Brandy and Kierstan. Driving through Rome to the airport, I don't want to listen to these girls so I grab my headphones and play "Let's Get Lost."

On the flight I realized I craved New York. Rome was nice but I was trying to escape all those thoughts of Sally, and now, John, there's this . . . thing. I have never been attracted to a man before. No fantasies. The movie on the flight, *Moulin Rouge* allowed me to forget about everything.

Kierstan walked past my row to go to the bathroom. I wanted off the plane. We landed and on the Manhattan-bound "A" train, New Yorkers had returned to rudeness. I realized I was going back home, back to Sally's. Back in Chinatown: the stench of raw fish, garbage everywhere, elderly Chinese women spitting every block.

The apartment was the exact mess I'd left. No sign of Jessica. I dropped my luggage and turned on the TV: anthrax deaths, the Yankees, NYFD hats everywhere. I found my cell phone. Two messages: one from Mom asking about the wedding, and one from Jez, "Let's rehearse and get drunk." I told Mom about the wedding, leaving John out, with nothing else to talk about.

I fell asleep in front of the TV.

The next day Jez and I met at Morrie's. I didn't want to play guitar. He showed me some songs he wrote. It was intricate, complicated stuff. I didn't even try. He asked me about Rome, I didn't know what to tell him. I hadn't told my Mom about John and I'm going to tell Jez? Someone I barely know? I didn't even really know what to tell. John was back in town and I hadn't called. I felt like I should. Just to get an understanding of the situation.

[You should write a song about Sally.] Yeah. I should. [What's wrong?] Nothing, just preoccupied. [Sally?] Yeah. No. When I was Rome I met this guy. [Who?] His name is John. He's an American. [What happened?] I, uh, slept with him. [You like guys?]

I took a sip of whiskey, and that was it. Jez didn't care. I felt better telling him. I didn't answer his question, but I felt better. I don't know the answer to the question.

[There's a lot of cool gay guys.] See I don't even know if I am. [It doesn't matter.] What do I tell my Mom? [Tell her you love her. That's all that really matters.]

Another round. Jez mentioned an upcoming gig at the Zinc Bar on Houston, and the possibility of a residency there. Two steady gigs a week would be great. Quilted Dreams. And another bar where we could drink for free. I ordered another and called John on my cell phone. He was drinking at a bar in Midtown and wanted me to come meet him. I walked into Gallagher's, past the meat lockers, and the photos of Joe DiMaggio, and John Lindsey, and he was there at the bar with an empty seat next to him. I sat down. No hugs, no kisses, no hands on knees. Just talk.

It's good to see you. [Yeah, you too.] How was Amsterdam? [Fine. I'm over that place. What are you drinking?] Jameson's.

He ordered one for me.

So what did you do in Amsterdam? [You know, the usual.] Is everything okay? [Oh yeah, sure.] You seem strange. [Do I?] Yeah. [. . . Tired.] Why did you invite me up here? [I wanted to see you.] And now that you've seen me? [What's the matter with you?] I am having trouble. [With what?] I'm still trying to figure out what's going on. [With what?] With me! [Oh, are we still talking about that?] How many people do you know have their first gay experience at my age? [It happens.] If you say so. [Tell me why you called me.] I don't know. [I do.] Okay, why did I call you? [Sex.] That's not true. [Of course it is. And it's fine. I love it. I want to have sex with you.] Is that all you want from me? [No.] Do you want to be in a relationship with me? [Oh my God, you are so adorable.] Why? [Is that what you want?] No, I don't know. Right now I want to understand what is going on. [I can tell you.] Please. [You are a gay man. We were attracted to each other, you had a little fling with Miss Kierstan which ended badly, and you came back to me. And you called me when I got back to town. You're gay, honey. Accept it. It's wonderful.]

I finished my drink and left. I walked to the subway. Alone. Riding the subway, I heard the echo of John's voice in my head, telling me, "You're gay, honey. Accept it." I got off the subway and walked to Sally's apartment. Her room the same mess, still that bra on the floor, pictures of us, from my first weekend in New York. Somehow there was one beer left in the 'fridge, which I opened and drank on the couch. I thought about Sally and picked up my guitar. I tried to write a chorus for her. My fingers ached. Nothing worked. I went for a walk.

Morrie's. Tonight, people gathered in front. As I neared, candles, huddled together, arms comforting each other, some cried, holding photos. Someone spray-painted "We love Jez" on a light pole.

Morrie grabbed me. [Oh my god, David, it's horrible; Jez was shot and killed.] What?! Where?! [In front of his apartment.] Who did this?! [His roommate saw the whole thing and called me from the hospital. He said a couple of kids tried to rob him and got scared.] Oh my God.

[How could this happen? I ow could this happen? What is wrong with people?]

I ordered a whiskey and drank it in one gulp. I ordered another. The room grew silent. A bearded man in his late 30s with blood stained on his shirt arrived. Jez's roommate. I didn't even know he had a roommate. Moving among the living, he was a ghost. Grief stained every cell in his body. He was witness to a wartime atrocity in the East Village. We are not prepared for this.

Back at Sally's, I called John. He told me he'd be there.

John hugged me and I began crying. John walked me into the bedroom and laid me down on the bed, and lay down with me. I was crying and I couldn't believe Jez was dead. I was crying and here I was in Sally's bed. With John. He wrapped his arms around me and kissed me. He brought me a tissue so I could blow my nose and a glass of water. I slept. I awoke later with John stroking my hair. I looked into his face and saw love.

Thank you. [Shhhhhh.]

Days passed. I was drinking Chopin vodka at Morrie's every day, again. Alone. I didn't talk to the bartenders or Morrie, just the glass, the booze, and the ice. Morrie let me keep the weekly gig. I got really good at blues tunes, but I wasn't making myself or anyone else feel better. And my drink was with me on stage, again. Once, I stopped in the middle of a song, Monk's "Crepuscule with Nellie" to take a swig. Friends to his Southampton home. John stopped returning my calls. I had my weekly gig and my Chopin vodka and that was my life. I tried to write a song about Jez but failed. I couldn't remember Jez or Sally.

I am on stage and I notice Ron, sitting at a table, alone near the back of the bar. I'm hazy drunk and play horribly. I'm done. Applause. I hate it. Let's Get Lost. Ron approaches me, buys me a drink. I sit with him. A few people tell me how much they like my music. I thank them, thinking they must be deaf. Ron takes a long swig from his drink.

[I have some bad news.] No. [I know.] What? [John's in the hospital.] Why? [Lymphoma.] He's gonna be okay. He'll fight it. [It's days, maybe weeks.]

I stand.

[Are you gonna be okay?] Yeah.

I walk through the East Village Gunfire, Lower East Side, Chinatown. Back home. Back to Sally's. Write a note. To whoever finds this: I have three friends and they're all dead. I loved them all. I'm sorry. David

I leave it on the desk . . . Great love for his many friends . . . I walk down the stairs out to the street. The Bridge. I'm going to the Bridge. I walk to the Brooklyn Bridge.

I am home. / I will jump from this bridge. / Let's get lost. / I wanna fuck you. / I am here. / Let's fuck. / Wartime atrocity / I don't wanna be fucked by you. / Am I home? / Ready am I? / Jez loved Mingus / Jez loved bourbon. / Went at it methodically / I loved Jez. / I'm going to walk Jez home and take a bullet with him. We will bleed together. / Escape outside himself / John made me laugh. / Here I am. / John gave me AIDS. / Home I am. / John fucked me without a condom. / I'm dead already. / I'm going to work at Windows on the World. / 7 AM Tuesday September 11th, 2001. / It's just not fair / Am I here? / I'm going to die with Sally. / I'm standing on this bridge. / The river. / Lights. / Horn. / I let go. / balance steady. / I am ready. / Now.

[*Cell phone chirps and chirps and chirps and chirps and chirps.*] Hi
Mom. [Hi honey, how are you?] I'm sad. [Everyone is sad.] Sally . . . [. . .
I know] John's eyes, full of love . . . [. . . I know, who's . . .] . . . Jez was
shot coming home from . . . [I need you.] I'm tired. [Come home.] I am
home.

It slips from my hand, into the water.

I watch it splash.

That is me.

There.

Is that me?

[*Very long beat. Back across the catwalk . . . A payphone . . .*] "*Hello
Operator . . . I'd like to make a collect call.*"

2 SOLDIERS

by Bathsheba Doran

CHARACTERS:

1412

1974

BATHSHEBA DORAN'S plays include *Odes and Gameshows* (The Camden Peple's Theatre), *Until Morning* (BBC Radio 4), *15 Minutes* (Edinburgh Festival), *The War Play* (Abingdon Theater), *The Parents' Evening* (Cherry Lane Theatre), and *Living Room in Africa*, which recently began development at the Eugene O'Neill Theater Center. Her adaptation of *Peer Gynt* was directed by Andrei Serban at the Theater of the Riverside Church in 2002. Current projects include adaptations of *Alice in Wonderland* for PACE University and of *Nathan the Wise* for Classic Stage Company. She is a playwriting fellow of The Juilliard School.

Some notes on the two soldiers: Although they are from different times and places, they have a total ease and familiarity with each other and their surroundings. The hill that they are sitting on it is covered with short grass. A beautiful spot on a warm afternoon.

1412 is standing, scouring the horizon. **1974** *is sitting, leaning back with his face up to the sun.*

1974: Still nothing?

1412: Nothing.

1974: Are you going to sit down now?

1412: No.

1974: I'm just sitting. They told me to wait here and I'm waiting. There's no point standing up when you're waiting. Is there? You don't want to talk?

1412: No.

1974: I'm bored, man.

1412: Why don't you read?

1974: A book? I can't ever concentrate on books.

1412: That's not good.

1974: Why not? You think it means something?

1412: Yes.

1974: What?

1412: It means you sound kind of dumb. That's not the kind of thing I would say out loud.

1974: You read a lot of books?

1412: Yes. A lot of books.

1974: I was thinking.

1412: About what?

1974: About the grass. About why it's so short. I was wondering if somebody mows it.

1412: It's short so we can see.

1974: See what?

1412: That nature has her ways.

1974: There was this one guy who was with us for a while. He read all the time. This one book he had. He'd finish up, start over. That's all he did. Never sat with us, never hung out, never partied, never played sports even if we were a guy short. Just went off by himself reading that stupid book.

1412: What book?

1974: I don't know I never read it. Maybe I'd know it if you told me the title.

1412: I don't know the title.

1974: Me neither. Whatever. So, Eddie, my buddy, he played this joke. We were all outside, and Jackson, the book guy, walked passed us, went over to his stuff, then he came back and he said: "any of you guys seen my book?" And Eddie said: "I hope you don't mind, I took it." And Jackson was kind of excited. He was always trying to tell us we should read this book and nobody ever gave two shits about it, then all of a sudden he's got Eddie telling him how he took the book and he had no idea that a book could give him such a great evening, you know? So Jackson's got this earnest look on his face, he just keeps nodding, with his eyes open real wide, all excited, like the two of them are going to have a really intense conversation about this book. And he says to Eddie: "so what in particular did you like about the book?" And Eddie just looked up at him, and grinned. And he held his hands out to the fire. Man, Jackson freaked out. We all just lost it. The look on his face. He just couldn't believe it, you know? That someone would burn his book. It was so outrageous. It was hysterical. [*No response.*] Two weeks later, this guy Eddie, he split open a goddamn donkey. Saw the animal in the rubble, flipped out, pulled out his knife and gutted it. He had to run after it too, but he caught it.

1412: Why he kill a donkey?

1974: Guess he figured it had no reason to be alive seeing as we lost like, seven, eight guys that day. You know? Peter, Mickey, Abner, Simmy, Dave, Davey Two, Jackson, Paulo, Frederick.

1412: That's bad.

1974: Sure.

1412: How they die?

1974: They fucked up the fucking grenade the fucking morons. It was a mess. Took a split second to figure out what had happened, and when the smoke cleared those guys were gone. They were just gone. And all there was this one grey donkey standing there in the rubble. It was fucking freaky. And then Eddie ran at it roaring. And he turned back to the three of us that were left and he was covered in blood, with this animal laid down by his feet. It was one of the most beautiful things I ever saw. You ever think men look beautiful?

1412: Yes.

1974: He had so much power, you know, and only a skinny old donkey to take it out on. He got sent home after that.

1412: Home?

1974: Boston.

1412: Where were you?

1974: Not in Boston, man. We don't fight at home. Not since . . . Jesus, not since the Indians.

1412: Where you fight?

1974: Away, mostly.

1412: No trouble at home?

1974: We got the police at home.

1412: They fight?

1974: They've got guns. And sticks.

1412: Sticks are good. A lot of training.

1974: And we've got boxing. And karate. Wrestling. But that's a totally different thing. People come to watch. And there's only two guys. You're not enemies, or nothing.

1412: Sometimes I think there is no enemy.

1974: Oh yeah? How d'you figure?

1412: Everybody wants the same thing.

1974: So?

1412: So everybody is the same.

1974: I don't think so, buddy. You want to be alive, they want you dead, you know what I mean?

1412: Yes.

1974: You want to live one way, they want to live another.

1412: Yes.

1974: So, you're not the same.

1412: Yes, same.

1974: It isn't the same.

1412: Yes, it is the same.

1974: Boy you can be pigheaded, anyone ever tell you that?

1412: Yes.

1974: Who?

1412: My wife.

1974: You're married?

1412: Sure.

1974: She thinks you're pigheaded?

1412: That's what she says.

1974: Well she's right. [*Pause.*] Why don't you take your hat off?

1412: Why should I?

1974: It's hot.

1412: So?

1974: So. You must be hot standing there.
1412: I don't take off my hat.

1974: Why?

1412: Unless circumstances insist.

1974: Circumstances do exist. It's hot. I'm taking my shirt off. [*He does.*] Eddie, Eddie never wore his shirt. Didn't matter what we were walking through, jungle, swamp, wouldn't wear his shirt. Got one hell of a suntan. He'd send pictures to his wife. She's write back to him, all this dirty stuff she wanted to do to him. He'd read it to us. We'd laugh our asses off. But Eddie, he really had a beautiful body. Not that I'm that way, or anything, but when he was just wearing cargo pants, and his dog tags, and his gun, he was really something to see. Like a fucking warrior. I like what you're wearing.

1412: Yes?

1974: Sure. Sort of noble.

1412: I like it.

1974: I wish I looked better in my uniform. I was excited when they gave it to me. And I got a picture taken of me in it, you know, that first day, for my mom. But it didn't come out so great. I looked kind of dumb.

1412: Kind of dumb, how?

1974: Young.

1412: You are young.

1974: I look better now. I'm a lot more built up. I might get a tattoo.

1412: That's nice.

1974: And I'm loving this sun. I bet when I get home I'm going to be all brown and ripped, you know, the girls are gonna go crazy. What do you think?

1412: Do I think you'll send the girls crazy?

1974: Yes.

1412: Horrible uniform.

1974: What do you mean? It's my uniform.

1412: I don't like it.

1974: Why not? It's cool. It's cool, bro.

1412: It's all one color. Why is it that muddy color?

1974: So people can't see you man. Look at you standing there with all those colors on the top of a hill. You're gonna get shot at.

1412: You think I'm going to get shot at?

1974: You're standing there like a peacock. That ain't smart. Sure you'll get shot at.

1412: I don't think so.

1974: Why?

1412: There's nobody coming. [*Pause.*]

1974: Is your sword heavy?

1412: Very heavy.

1974: Can I try it?

1412: No.

1974: Just for a second?

1412: No.

1974: C'mon.

1412: It's my sword.

1974: So.

1412: So it has my energy in it.

1974: Excuse me?

1412: My energy, from my body, run through metal. Your energy would confuse it.

1974: It would confuse it? The sword's not alive, man. It isn't going to make any difference to the sword if I touch it.

1412: Yes it makes a difference. It is my sword.

1974: It's cool man. You don't want me to touch it, I won't touch it. Some people are really personal about their shit. Fine, I won't touch it.

1412: No.

1974: I just said I won't touch it.

1412: No, *I* said you won't touch it.

1974: Meaning?

1412: What?

1974: Meaning?

1412: I said.

1974: I agreed. So it wasn't just your decision.

1412: Why you keep talking?

1974: Why not? I'm bored man. If I wanted to I'd touch your sword. I'm sitting here with a great big gun.

1412: So?

1974: So if I want to touch your sword, I'm going to touch it.

1412: But you don't touch another man's sword. What is wrong with you?

1974: Says who?

1412: Everybody knows it.

1974: Everybody who?

1412: Everybody.

1974: I don't think so.

1412: Why you want to touch it?

1974: To see if it's heavy.

1412: I told you it's heavy.

1974: I want to see for myself.

1412: Only time you touch another man's sword is with another sword. Or after you killed him.

1974: The way I fight, there aren't rules, friend. That's the way I fight, so . . . I do what the fuck I please. So just because you've got rules, don't be thinking I'm going to follow them. Element of surprise. How's there supposed to be an element of surprise if we're following rules the whole time?

1412: I don't know. Why you need surprise?

1974: To win.

1412: You don't need surprise to win. Just to be better fighter.

1974: That's part of being a good fighter. Strategy.

1412: No. Is politician. I am not politician. I don't like politicians.

1974: Me neither. I'm a good fighter. How long have you been training?

1412: Since five.

1974: Five years old?

1412: I got uniform when I was fifteen.

1974: The army gave me this. You really don't like the color, huh?

1412: No. [*A beat.*]

1974: You want me to take over?

1412: What do you mean?

1974: You sit, I watch. You must be tired.

1412: No.

1974: Well I'm going keep watch as well. [*He stands up and also scours the horizon.*] It's all clear.

1412: Really?

1974: You're right, dude. Just because we can't seen anything doesn't mean they're not there. [*He spins around.*] There's nothing behind us.

1412: That's good.

1974: Do you think we should just wait?

1412: I was told to wait here. I wait.

1974: Yeah, but maybe we're meant to take initiative, you know?

1412: Like what?

1974: Are there any trees? We could climb a tree. Then we'd be hidden and the enemy might come out.

1412: There are no trees.

1974: You couldn't climb a tree. Not dressed like that. You see me, I'm ready for anything. I can run, I can climb, I can wade through water. I don't know how you can even move, dressed like that.

1412: Why you want to wade through water?

1974: I don't want to. You might have to.

1412: I don't wade through water.

1974: You'd drown, all that shit you're wearing. How can you move?

1412: I can move.

1974: Not as fast as me, I bet. That's the thing about me, I'm really fast. I got a nickname. You want to know what it is?

1412: Sure.

1974: Speedy. Speedy Gonzales. You know who that is?

1412: That's you.

1974: That's right. That's me. You got a nickname?

1412: A special name?

1974: Right. Did the boys give you a special name?

1412: No.

1974: Oh that's too bad, man. Do you feel bad about it?

1412: Why should I?

1974: Because it's a term of affection, you know. Like being in a club.

1412: I am not in a club.

1974: Sure you are. You're a soldier, man. You want me to give you a name.

1412: No.

1974: You sure?

1412: Yes.

1974: I'm gong to give you a name. How about . . .

1412: I don't need a name.

1974: I'm going to call you The Head.

1412: The Head?

1974: Sure, because you're all upright and shit. Like a headmaster. What do you think? The Head?

1412: I like it.

1974: Good.

1412: The Head.

1974: That's right. You want to hold my gun?

1412: Why?

1974: I just thought you might want to look at it. I'm generous like that.

1412: Alright. [*He takes the gun.* **1974** *shows him how to point it.*] Does it shoot very far?

1974: Oh very far. Hundreds of miles. Maybe a thousand from here. Could be.

1412: You've shot many people with it?

1974: I don't know. It shoots so far you can't really see. And there's lots of people shooting so you can't really tell whose is whose. We work like a team.

1412: I see.

1974: We all shoot together. Then we all walk forward together. Can I have the sword?

1412: You said you weren't going to ask about the sword.

1974: I thought maybe after you touched the gun . . .

1412: Nobody else touches the sword.

1974: You're really selfish, you know that. Maybe I'm going to call you Big Head.

1412: Why?

1974: You're really arrogant.

1412: Arrogant is good. Proud.

1974: It's rude.

1412: Is important to take pride in self. Otherwise what do you stand for? Look at you. You don't dress nice, you don't stand nice and tall. You're a mess.

1974: Maybe I'm going to call you Pig Head, what about that? That's funny. Because you're pig headed, you know, like your wife was saying? How do you like that? Pig Head?

1412: I don't like it.

1974: So don't be rude.

1412: I like The Head.

1974: Okay then. You got to earn your nickname. Give me back my gun. [*He gives it back.*] Can I try on your hat? Oh c'mon. Just for a second. [**1412** *gives it to him.*]

1412: Is not good to share hat. Is my hat. You're a lot of work, you know that? Always have to keep you entertained.

1974: Man, this is heavy.

1412: Yes.

1974: This is really heavy. Doesn't it hurt your neck?

1412: Not any more.

1974: Same as me. First time I picked up that backpack, I thought I was going to die, man. When they woke me up and said we were going on a fifteen-mile hike, I wished we were in the middle of a battle and that I would get shot immediately so I could fall down dead and somebody would take off the fucking thing. But now I can go for twice that.

1412: The weather is really nice today.

1974: Yes. Better without the hat, huh?

1412: Alright, give it back now. [**1974** *hands it back.*]

1974: My gun's pretty heavy, too, isn't it.

1412: Guns are easy.

1974: No. You have to learn how to put them together. And to aim.

1412: To point.

1974: You weren't even holding it right. It's not as easy as it looks. You know the best place to get shot? In the butt. Then you can go home.

1412: But then you lose.

1974: Not everybody goes home.

1412: But you lose.

1974: Whatever, man. If you can go home, you should go home.

1412: Then why you go at all?

1974: Don't you want to go home? [*Pause.*] What exactly did they say to you?

1412: Go up onto the hill.

1974: Me too.

1412: Alright then.

1974: So we're just going to wait?

1412: I have to wait. Why you keep bothering me?

1974: Do you think we're meant to fight each other?

1412: Nobody said we should fight.

1974: I know, but take initiative, you know.

1412: You don't have a sword.

1974: I know. I'd win.

1412: You don't know. You never had to fight anyone up close, right? Is very different.

1974: I guess it's all about the element of surprise. If I just took my gun out when you weren't expecting it.

1412: That's why there are rules. That's not a fight. That's murder. Different thing.

1974: Not if it's part of a war.

1412: Anyone can murder anyone. Doesn't mean anything.

1974: Okay. What about a fist fight?

1412: No.

1974: You chicken?

1412: No. I wasn't told to fight.

1974: Oh come on man. No one's gonna know.

1412: I'll know.

1974: So?

1412: I obey orders. They do strategy.

1974: Aren't you bored?

1412: Yes. What about word game?

1974: You want to play a word game?

1412: Sure.

1974: I'm no good at word games.

1412: I spy with my little eye, something beginning with S.

1974: Sky? Soldiers?

1412: No.

1974: Sss-sword?

1412: No.

1974: What? What?

1412: Space! You lose. I spy with my little eye, something beginning with S.

1974: Is it any of those other words? This is really boring. This is more boring than before. Let's have a fight. I think we're supposed to have a fight.

1412: Not good enough reason. Why don't you just sit and think like before?

1974: I can't think of anything to think about.

1412: Doesn't surprise me.

1974: Are you thinking?

1412: How can I think when you keep talking? [*Pause.*]

1974: Are you thinking now?

1412: No.

1974: Why not?

1412: Nothing came in.

1974: You see? Me neither. How can the mind be empty? That never happens. I guess it's kind of relaxing.

1412: That's right. Relax. Be quiet.

1974: Why? Are you going to kill me?

1412: Why you say that?

1974: You're standing there with an enormous sword. And I don't want to fall asleep with an enormous sword and wake up with my head chopped off. I'm not going to relax. I'm going to stand here just like you and my hand's on my gun.

1412: Okay.

1974: So we'll just stand here. [*They do.*] I just don't want to be standing up.

1412: So sit.

1974: Not with you standing there like that.

1412: Your decision.

1974: Listen, Head, I'm really tired. Can't we both just sit down. For a minute. Take half time, you know what I mean?

1412: I'm not allowed.

1974: You're not allowed? Says who?

1412: My superiors.

1974: There not here, are they? They can't see.

1412: You can sit down. I'm not going to hurt you. [**1974** *sits down.*]

1974: I really want you to sit down with me.

1412: I can't. It is a sign of defeat.

1974: Not to me. I'm the only one here.

1412: We don't know that.

1974: How long are you going to stand for?

1412: Until I fall down.

1974: Hey you want me to knock you down? Then you could sit for a bit but it wouldn't be your fault.

1412: No. Is cheating.

1974: It was just a suggestion.

1412: I don't cheat.

1974: Am I getting a tan?

1412: No. You haven't changed color.

1974: I bet you're really, tired.

1412: I don't get tired.

1974: Liar.

1412: Am not tired yet.

1974: Okay then. That's good. We'll just wait.

1412: Okay then. We're waiting.

1974: Goddamn it, will you just sit down with me?

1412: No.

1974: Sit down! [*Pointing the gun.*] I've got a gun to your head.

1412: Why you always want to murder?

1974: Who mows the lawn here? Who looks after it? Maybe that's who we'll see next. The man who mows the lawn. Someone has to. Why else would the grass be short? Do you see anything?

1412: Nothing.

1974: You'll let me know?

1412: Yes.

1974: We're on the same side right?

1412: I don't know.

1974: But nobody said fight, right.

1412: Nobody said fight.

1974: That's nice. You think we're winning out there?

1412: Oh yes. We always win.

1974: Yes. They said go. Go onto the hill. I didn't ask any questions because you're not supposed to ask any questions.

1412: That's right. They said go.

1974: They said go. [*He stands up, ready with his gun to face the enemy. They wait. End of play.*]

DAVY AND STU

by anton dudley

CHARACTERS:

Davy: Male, 14

Stu: Male, 15

SETTING:

A field on a hill. A Southern Island
in the Orkney Island chain, Scotland.

ANTON DUDLEY received his MFA from NYU's Tisch School of the
Arts and BA from Vassar College. His plays, including *Slag Heap, The
Lake's End, Honor and the River, This Ball of Mud and Fire, Soul
Perversions, Bleeding the Leech,* and *Spamlet* have been produced in
six states. Mr. dudley has received developmental fellowships from
Manhattan Theatre Club, New York Theatre Workshop, the Cherry
Lane Theatre, New York Stage & Film, and the Dramatists Guild of
America. He currently teaches playwriting at Adelphi University and
serves as both the literary manager for Cherry Red Productions and the
director of the Fellowship Program for the Dramatists Guild.

A Southern Island in the Orkney's. A few ruined monoliths. DAVY, *14,* and STU, *15, are at the edge of a bog. It is starting to go dark.*

DAVY: I was dreaming I was a child in your arms.

STU: Yeah?

DAVY: Yeah.

STU: That's one dream I don't think will ever come true.

DAVY: Suppose not . . . S'just a thought.

STU: How's your mother?

DAVY: Good. Is your cat still alive?

STU: We put her down last night.

DAVY: S'that why you weren't here, then?

STU: Yeah. My sister was all crying and I had to sit up with her, 'case she had nightmares.

DAVY: Where was your mother?

STU: She works on Monday nights.

DAVY: Aye. I forgot. We only buy food on the weekend.

STU: Stupid. That's when everybody shops. The lines're too long. You and your Mum should go on Mondays. Say hello to my mother. They used to be friends.

DAVY: Yeah, before she was with my Dad.

STU: No, he was with her.

DAVY: What do you mean? They were together.

STU: Yeah, well, your Dad's the one with the reputation, isn't he?

DAVY: Whichever way, my mother isn't too happy about it. S'probably why we only shop on the weekend.

STU: Is he still in grocery, your Dad?

DAVY: No. When he left town, he joined the ironworks in Glasgow. Last I heard.

STU: Ah.

DAVY: Did you bring minty chewing gum?

STU: No.

DAVY: I asked you to bring minty chewing gum.

STU: Get your own.

DAVY: Your mother gets it cheap, though. You promised.

STU: Well, I forgot.

DAVY: It's just . . .

STU: I didn't bring any minty chewing gum. [*Pause.*]

DAVY: . . . And if you say you're going to meet me at four, then you should be here at four.

STU: Did I keep you waiting, then?

DAVY: Yes, you did.

STU: Well, aren't you just an impatient little Hoover.

DAVY: That's not what I meant.

STU: Are you scared of old Jenny Green Teeth? Think she's lurking about in the bog, do you?

DAVY: No.

STU: Aye, y'are. Think she's going to grab onto your ankles and pull you screaming into the bog, chew you up and spit you out like a little heap of peat moss?

DAVY: Look, it's going dark early and I just don't like it.

STU: But you still waited.

DAVY: That should make you happy.

STU: Aye, it does. [*Pause.*] Look at your little rosy cheeks, like a dumpling, you are; Jenny Green Teeth'd be salivating at the sight of you.

DAVY: Stop on about Jenny Green Teeth!

STU: Ah, you're a little boy. [STU *kneels, sitting back on his heels.*] Go on, then.

DAVY: Don't know that I can now, thinking about her crawling out the bog.

STU: It's not true, Davy, it's just a story.

DAVY: It's not just a story. What about Bobby Denim? Hm? What about him? Gone off and played in the marshes and he never came home.

STU: So?

DAVY: So, they found his woolly cap covered in green ooze, that's so.

STU: 'Cause it had been in the bog for two weeks, what d'ya think it would have looked like?

DAVY: Aye, but don't you think it's a bit strange they never found his body? Only his cap. And you know what they say. Jenny Green Teeth pulls little boys into the bog and eats them there, then flosses her teeth with their dark brown hair. That's what they say. That's why all they found was his cap.

STU: I think you're talking a load of rubbish.

DAVY: I think Bobby Denim would disagree.

STU: Bobby Denim was a nasty little prat who probably got what was coming to him; with or without the help of one Jenny Green Teeth. Look, it's getting dark, now. If you want to get home before the sun does, I suggest we go.

DAVY: Didn't you bring the torch?

STU: Of course, I did. I've got further to go than you.

DAVY: I wish we could go to my house.

STU: We will when we're older. When you're running the grocery and living on Beekham Hill Road.

DAVY: I'll never run the grocery.

STU: Why not?

DAVY: I'm going to live in a city; where there's always lights on. Where you can always hear other people.

STU: Don't get privacy in a city.

DAVY: I don't think you need privacy in a city. No one cares. You can stand in the middle of the street, starkers, and be perfectly invisible. The country's inhabited by Nosey Parkers but the city, they've got other things to worry about—like their own lives.

STU: Yeah, well, you be sure to visit me out here, slopping the pigs' dinner out on my farm. Won't catch me in no bloody city.

DAVY: Going to have yourself a pair of oversized welly-boots and a flock of sheep, are you?

STU: Where'd you get language like that? I'll box your bloody ears in. [*They wrestle.* STU *gets* DAVY *in a head lock.*]

DAVY: Hey, hey, hey. Okay, okay. You win.

STU: Who's the strongest?

DAVY: Get off!

STU: Who's the strongest!

DAVY: You are.

STU: Say it, say Stu's the strongest.

DAVY: Stu's the strongest. Now get off, you're hurting me.

STU: You're soft, you are. [STU *climbs off* DAVY. *Pause.*]

DAVY: Stu?

STU: What?

DAVY: Did you take a bath after school? S'that why you weren't here at four?

STU: I was filthy. The rugby field was muddy.

DAVY: But you're always filthy. S'why they call you Filthy Stu.

STU: Hey! I'll bloody box your ears again.

DAVY: I don't care; I've never mentioned it before.

STU: Then why're you on about it, now?

DAVY: I just thought it strange you had a bath after school. Wanted to know why.

STU: 'Cause I felt like being clean. Why else d'ya have a bath?

DAVY: Bet your mother wasn't too happy, turning the immersion heater on in the middle of the day—using up all her hot water.

STU: Well, she wasn't home, was she? Probably down in Glasgow for the night with your Father.

DAVY: Shut up.

STU: S'getting a bit dark. I'll put the torch on to scare away old Jenny Green Teeth, shall I?

DAVY: Oh, she doesn't come out at night.

STU: No?

DAVY: No, at night she sleeps at the bottom of the bog, scraping the bones of the little boys she's ate during the day. She files them down with a little piece of flint and then builds traps with them to catch little girls and rabbits and moles and sheep. When the boys hear them screaming they run to the marshes to set them free and then Jenny Green Teeth'll pull those boys into the bog and feast on them . . .

STU: So, we can stay out here all night, then—if Jenny's busying herself with making cages and traps.

DAVY: No, 'cause at night comes the Tarkswold Troll.

STU: The what?

DAVY: Where've you been, Stu? Were you never told the stories when you were younger?

STU: No, I was too busy slopping the pig feed and shaving the sheep. Cutting the heads off rabbits so's your mother could have a dinner on your table. Anyways, I have to say I'm not regretting it—I can't very well be afraid of what I don't know about, can I?

DAVY: But you can't be ready for it, either, if you don't know about it.

STU: I don't think I have to worry about being ready for no Tarkswold Troll, Davy. And if you're so scared, you needn't be. I'm strong enough to beat him off you.

DAVY: Yeah, I suppose you are.

STU: Well don't suppose, know it as truth.

DAVY: Yeah, I do.

STU: Well, good. [**DAVY** *touches* **STU***'s chest.*]

DAVY: Stu?

STU: What's that?

DAVY: You smell real nice . . . Thank you. [*The sky goes dark.*]

PERFECT

by Mary Gallagher

CHARACTERS:

Tina

Kitty

Dan

Binky

All the characters are in their late 30s.

TIME:

The present, after dinner.

PLACE:

A hallway or pantry at **TINA** and **BINKY's**
place, with something to put stuff on and
something to perch or lean on.

MARY GALLAGHER is a playwright, screenwriter, and novelist whose
plays are produced throughout the United States and in many other
countries. Many of them are published by Dramatists Play Service,
including *Father Dreams, How to Say Goodbye, Dog Eat Dog, Win/
Lose/Draw* (co-written by Ara Watson), *De Donde?*, and *Windshook*. Ms.
Gallagher's new full-length plays are *I Know You're the One* and *4YOR-
LUV*. Her many screenplays include *Bonds of Love* (CBS, 1993), which
starred Treat Williams, and *The Passion of Ayn Rand* (Showtime, 1999),
for which Helen Mirren won the Emmy. Ms. Gallagher's awards and
honors include a Guggenheim, a Rockefeller, three NEAs, a NYFA, a
Writers Guild Award, and a Berrilla Kerr Award. She is currently writing
two novels: a contemporary comic romance called *Leaving without
Leaving*, and an untitled historical romance.

TINA *and* BINKY *are entertaining* KITTY *and* DAN, *who have never met before.* BINKY *is not seen. Footsteps are heard, two pairs of high heels.* TINA *enters, followed by* KITTY, *both carrying dinner dishes which they plunk down as they talk.*

TINA: So wadaya think?

KITTY: So far, he's fine—

TINA: I think he is perfect!

KITTY: He's great-looking, that's for sure—

TINA: My God, Kitty, I'm drooling! And smart, he's like Joe Genius at the law firm, Binky says—

KITTY: He seems like he's bright, he's read a book lately, at least—

TINA: He reads like a maniac. Like at the office, Binky says everybody's talking about who would want to try out for "Survivor: The Galapagos," and Dan is like, "You know I was reading this book last night," and everyone goes, "Oh." But I mean, you love that.

KITTY: But he's funny too. I mean I think he's said a lot of funny things tonight—

TINA: Are you kidding? God, he is hysterical! He gets Binks laughing on the phone, like Binks can't stop, like with tears—

KITTY: And he offered to help clear the table.

TINA: That, I could not believe.

KITTY: Of course, he is a guest—

TINA: But still. They won't, you know?

KITTY: It's like the last bastion, the Alamo—

TINA: Or even if they did it for some brief exciting era, now it's over. You get up, you pick up a plate, and they dig in, they get this look, this rigid look . . .

KITTY: Sort of daunted, but entrenched . . .

TINA: And they start talking sports.

KITTY: Or corporate talk. "To the best of my knowledge, Fred."

TINA: Right! Right! That's the best thing about Binky being Binky. When people start that crap with him, it just doesn't cut it. "To the best of my knowledge, Binky . . ." [*They start giggling. They lean on each other, giggling.* **DAN** *enters.*]

DAN: Hey.

TINA: Hey.

KITTY: Hey.

DAN: You guys are having a good time in here. Binks and I are missing it. We feel ripped off. We feel we should express that.

KITTY: And we're glad you did. [*He keeps looking at her for a beat. There is clearly a strong mutual attraction. They are faintly smiling.* **TINA** *enjoys this. Then:*]

DAN: Also, Binky sent me to inquire, I quote, "What is the coffee situation?"

TINA: It's working, tell him. What's he think this is, the Dog 'n Suds?

DAN: Uh . . .

TINA: He's the one that bought the espresso-maker, so he's gotta learn to wait. Tell him to pretend he's in, you know, whatsit—

KITTY: & DAN: Tuscany.

TINA: Tuscany.

DAN: How 'bout if I tell him it's almost ready?

KITTY: "To the best of my knowledge, Binky."

DAN: [*Grins.*] "Just an estimate, based on available data—we'll crunch more numbers, Binks." [DAN *exits. They listen for a beat till he's gone. Then* TINA *pokes* KITTY.]

TINA: [*About the vibes.*] WOO!

KITTY: Yeah. It's great. So far.

TINA: What is this "so far"? There is no hidden horror. Trust me. I told you, I looked into him. Not only is he not attached, he has the perfect history. He was married once, so he's not afraid of commitment. But they were really young and it just didn't work out. But they're still friends, he even plays squash with her new husband, so clearly he's not bitter. But, they've been divorced for years, and he's dated a lot and lived with two other women, so he's not hung up on her. No kids, so there is no issue of "maybe his kids will hate you." But he has one nephew and two nieces and he adores them, so he's not opposed to kids. Plus he doesn't smoke, he drinks like just enough, he gets loose but not sloppy, and he'll smoke some dope if someone passes it around, but he doesn't buy dope and even when he smokes it, he never turns into an asshole. I mean, if you don't take him, take Binky and I'll take him!

KITTY: I really am attracted to him—

TINA: Tell me about it! It's like . . . a force!

KITTY: Yeah?

TINA: Yeah! Also you keep grinning.

KITTY: I do? Oh God—

TINA: You both do. Me and Binky feel left out.

KITTY: God, how embarrassing—

TINA: So what's the hold-up?

KITTY: [*Beat, then:*] You're gonna get pissed off.

TINA: I might, I'll tell ya. I oughta get anointed Queen for coming up with him. Or Pope. 'Cause do you know what's <u>out there</u>?

KITTY: I know, I know, believe me . . . okay. Look at the evidence. He's a corporate lawyer. He makes a lot of money.

TINA: It's not that great, he makes like what Binky makes—

KITTY: Compared to say the average income of the average working—

TINA: Okay, okay, right—

KITTY: He drives a BMW. He went to Fiji on vacation. He makes jokes about his investment portfolio, but he <u>has</u> a portfolio and he's only, what? Thirty-six?

TINA: Thirty-eight. That's better, men are assholes till they're thirty-eight. See, he's even thirty-eight! <u>What are you afraid of</u>?

KITTY: Who do you think he voted for?

TINA: [*Stopped; then stalls for time.*] Huh?

KITTY: I knew it!

TINA: No no, wait, hold on—

KITTY: God, it's all so <u>depressing</u>—

TINA: No, wait a minute, we don't know—

KITTY: You know, you know in your heart—

TINA: I don't! You never know. Binky's just the same as Dan, he's practically a clone of Dan, and Binky didn't vote for him—

KITTY: That's because you told him if he voted for him, he would not get laid for four more years.

TINA: But he wouldn't've done it anyway, Binky never really votes for them. Sometimes, yeah, he talks the talk, just to get me all wound up, but "once inside the booth," you know—

KITTY: This is denial, Tina.

TINA: No! Even when Reagan died, the Great Communicator and the state funeral and all, and everyone kept saying, "Ronald Reagan made us feel good about ourselves again," and then they'd play these sound-bites from his speeches? And Binky said, "Tina, listen to his voice, he sounds like a child molester." [*Doing creepy Reagan.*] "Come with me, little girl, it's morning in America . . ."

KITTY: Yeah, yeah . . . we can all sneer and laugh at them, but do you think they care? They sell yo-yos in the gift shop of the Ronald Reagan Presidential Library, yo-yos with Ronald Reagan's name on them, that's how much they care.

TINA: All I'm saying is, Binky doesn't vote for them—

KITTY: It's how Dan votes that worries me!

TINA: Well, I don't think it's fair. For you to just . . . assume . . .

KITTY: I bet Binky knows.

TINA: [*Lying.*] . . . I don't think they talk politics.

KITTY: Get Binky and I'll ask him.

TINA: Oh, great, that's great! Why don't you just ask Dan? Go ahead, just . . . [*Throws up hands.*]

KITTY: [*Bleakly.*] Because if he votes for them, I'll cry, or puke, or something . . .

TINA: [*Beat; then, gently.*] Look. Why don't you wait. You know? Enjoy it for a while. You guys could have so much fun. And he could be the greatest lover in America. Don't ruin it before you even—

KITTY: No, I can't face falling for him, getting suckered in, but all the time suspecting, probing, and then finding out! No. I'd rather end it now. One clean . . . [*Chopping motion.*] I'll go back in, I'll ask him. [KITTY *turns to exit.* TINA *grabs her.*]

TINA: Now, damnit, Kitty! This is really self-destructive. I don't think you <u>want</u> to have a good relationship. Or even a good time! I think . . . I think, and I am serious, you are <u>avoiding</u> real live men—

KITTY: No! There are certain things—principles, gut instincts, call them what you will—that every person has to cling to. That's what makes us who we are. I would not ask <u>you</u> to give up the deepest convictions that you have—

TINA: [*Annoyed.*] Name one!

KITTY: —and you would not want <u>me</u> to throw away my most dearly-held beliefs—

TINA: I want you to have a nice man in your life! I want you to be happy!

KITTY: . . . Yeah, I know. And I want that too, I do! But I can't stand the way this country's going. And if I can't stop it, at least I won't participate. I won't have sex with anyone who votes for them.

TINA: [*Beat, then, flatly.*] You're talking about every man who makes a decent living—

KITTY: No!

TINA: Well, the vast majority—

KITTY: "The majority," that just means "more than half." And last time they didn't even get <u>half</u>! Bush, that smirking, squinchy-eyed— you'd kill yourself if your blind date turned out to be <u>him</u>—<u>he</u> only got in because his brother's flunkies blinded senior citizens and would- n't let black people vote!

TINA: Oh God, here we go . . .

KITTY: Not to mention all the people who stopped voting <u>years</u> ago, because they were too weak and wasted, <u>drained</u>, from all those years of <u>rage</u> at Reagan and Old Bad Bush and Ollie North and Newt Gingrich and Trent Lott and Henry Hyde and Antonin Scalia and—

TINA: Look, don't ask Dan tonight, okay? We don't need a bloodbath here.

KITTY: —Cheney, Rumsfeld, Ashcroft, Rice—

TINA: Whoa, didn't you just skip eight years? Clinton was one of ours. And the guy would screw a cantaloupe.

KITTY: But he didn't try to give away the arctic wilderness! He didn't call an education bill "No Child Left Behind" and then cut the funding for it! He didn't bring back Star Wars and gag orders for birth control and trillion dollar deficits! He didn't lock up immigrants for years just "on suspicion," without lawyers or human rights! He didn't attack a <u>country</u> just so he could carve it up and hand the pieces to his friends and act like no one died! Clinton broke our hearts, but getting blowjobs at the office is not the same as genocide! And Clinton could speak in sentences, with clauses. He could sustain a complex thought! Bush is a vacuum, a black hole, I'm surprised the Lincoln bed doesn't get sucked into him— [DAN *enters.* KITTY *shuts up. They look at each other, slowly start smiling.* TINA *grins.*]

TINA: I think the coffee's ready. [TINA *exits.*]

DAN: Want to have dinner tomorrow night?

KITTY: [*Beat, then blurts.*] Did you vote for Bush?

DAN: [*Surprised.*] Actually, I didn't vote. Terrible, I know. But the firm sent me to Kuwait with one day's notice, so I didn't have time to do the absentee ballot thing.

KITTY: Oh . . . huh . . . [*She's more torn: can she let it go at this? She and* DAN *slowly move toward each other as:*] I would like to have dinner with you.

DAN: Great.

KITTY: I really want to have sex with you.

DAN: Fantastic. [*They move into their first kiss. But* KITTY *breaks it, she can't help herself.*]

KITTY: But if you <u>had</u> voted, who would you have voted for? [*Blackout. End of play.*]

WHITE RUSSIAN

by Joseph Goodrich

This play is for Mick Collins.

CHARACTERS:

Adriana

Katja

Wynton

TIME:

A foreign country.

The preferred pace is adagio.

JOSEPH GOODRICH is a writer and actor from Minnesota. His plays have been produced in New York City, Los Angeles, San Francisco, New Orleans, Minneapolis/Saint Paul, and Portland, Maine. His *Steak Knife Bacchae* is included in *Padua: Plays from the Padua Hills Playwrights Festival* (Padua Hills Publications, distributed by TCG). *Captain 11* and *My Pants* are published by Playscripts, Inc. Mr. Goodrich's poetry has appeared in the *Venice West Review*, his fiction in *Bullet* magazine, and he was a contributor to *Conducting a Life: Reflections on the Theatre of Maria Irene Fornes*. His work runs the gamut from opera libretti (*The Art of Eating*, music by Jeffrey Lependorf) to comic books ("Human Interest," written for Marvel Comics' *Spider-Man Unlimited* series).

Mr. Goodrich is a member of New Dramatists, the Mystery Writers of America, the Screen Actors' Guild, and Actors' Equity Association.

1.

Darkness. Distant, distorted rumbling. Lights up. ADRIANA, *face in hands.* WYNTON *watches her. Rumbling fades. Silence. A clock chimes ten times.* WYNTON *checks his watch. Silence.* ADRIANA *looks up.*

ADRIANA: Forgive me. It's just so . . .

WYNTON: It's all right.

ADRIANA: . . . Horrible. [*Pause.*]

WYNTON: Does Katja know?

ADRIANA: I'm afraid she does, yes.

WYNTON: How did she take it?

ADRIANA: It was a great shock to her.

WYNTON: Understandably.

ADRIANA: I tried to keep it from her. God knows I tried. [*Pause.*] Find them, Wynton. Promise me you'll find them and do to them what they did to Allegra.

WYNTON: My dear, that's not for me—

ADRIANA: They broke her legs, Wynton. They gouged out her eyes. They sliced her belly open and filled her with shit. Their own, I imagine. Then they tossed her on the steps and ran away. Laughing with delight, no doubt. Promise me you'll find them and do to them what they did to her.

WYNTON: I can't promise that, Adriana. You know that. [*Pause.*] Why don't you move into town? It's not safe out here anymore. Doesn't this prove it?

ADRIANA: Rubbish.

WYNTON: Move into town, Adriana, and have done with it. [*Pause.*]

ADRIANA: I want you to find them, Wynton. I want you to find them and kill them and bring them here. Then I too shall laugh with <u>delight</u> —as I feed their corpses to my new dog . . . And when my new dog has finished feasting, when my new dog has licked the last drop of blood off the steps—then I'll move into town. [*Pause.* KATJA *enters.*] We're busy now, dear. Could you come back later? [KATJA *starts to exit.*]

WYNTON: Stay, Katja. This concerns you, too. [*She stops.*] If you won't think of yourself, think of Katja. Be sensible, my dear.

ADRIANA: Leave her out of this.

WYNTON: Do you want to watch her die, too?

KATJA: Watch me what?

ADRIANA: I asked you to leave her out of this!

WYNTON: Could you watch her die?

ADRIANA: Wynton!

WYNTON: Could you?

ADRIANA: Wynton—please!

WYNTON: Katja—could you watch Adriana die?

KATJA: I don't know what—

ADRIANA: NO ONE IS GOING TO WATCH ANYONE DIE! WILL YOU PLEASE FOR THE LOVE OF GOD CHANGE THE SUBJECT! [*Silence.*] The Captain is trying to convince us to leave, darling. He says we'll be safer elsewhere. He fears for our safety. He's rather more concerned with future contingencies than with present actualities. Perhaps the here and now is simply beyond his ken. Perhaps he is too exclusively concerned with the exquisite. It happens, you know. Look at poor old Mills. He's been polishing agates for years. His sensibilities are so refined I'm surprised he still has a shadow. He's atrophied terribly here. Physically. He can't breathe at all well and he gives off the sweet rotting-apple smell of the hopeless diabetic. Have you seen him recently?

WYNTON: They've killed Del. [*Pause.*]

ADRIANA: They've what?

WYNTON: Del was murdered on Thursday night. [*Silence.*]

ADRIANA: That's impossible. I saw Del just the other evening. We both saw him. Didn't you see him just the other evening, Katja?

KATJA: Thursday night, actually.

ADRIANA: There you have it.

KATJA: I spoke to him for what must have been a quarter of an hour. At the very least. You saw me, didn't you, Danny? Me with Del?

ADRIANA: I assure you I did. No, Del is still very much in and of this world, I can tell you that.

WYNTON: I've see the body, Adriana. I have photographs.

ADRIANA: Photographs of your dog! [*Silence.*]

KATJA: No—I spoke to Del for a good quarter of an hour. It was Del I was speaking to, of that I'm certain. Same wry smile and receding hairline. Del as ever was, if you ask me. [*Pause.*] Of course we've never been what one could call fast friends, but—and I told him this in the course of our conversation—I know you . . . Del . . . as well as anyone in our community, and I've heard the stories making the rounds, and I find not a shred of correspondence between the man they portray and the man standing in front of me. A man we've all known and loved for years. [*Pause.*]

ADRIANA: I spoke to him just before you did, do you know that? Madeleine had slipped into her gray evening gown and was stirring a pitcher of Gibtinis for all and sundry. James was reading aloud from an article he found of enormous interest. Mills was quite severely sunburned and flaking all over the Persian. A perfectly normal evening, pressed from the same mold as hundreds of evenings before. And into this . . . oasis of calm . . . Del made his entrance.

KATJA: I saw him. He was out of breath.

ADRIANA: He'd been running.

KATJA: For his health.

ADRIANA: We sat and had a lovely talk and then he patted my thigh and tipped me the wink and said he'd best start mingling or Bitsy would pitch a wobbly. He must have gone straight to you.

KATJA: Or very shortly afterwards, yes.

WYNTON: And what did Del have to say?

KATJA: Why . . . Nothing of consequence.

ADRIANA: You know Del.

KATJA: He was worried about the strike.

WYNTON: Did he tell you that?

KATJA: He didn't have to. It was obvious. [*Pause.*]

WYNTON: Anything else?

ADRIANA: I know you'll find this hard to believe, but after our conversation, I . . . It all breaks down for me there. I find I'm completely incapable of reconstructing the evening from that point onward. I no longer have the strength of will to follow the chain of succeeding events.

KATJA: That's my situation exactly. [*Silence. A car horn sounds.*]

WYNTON: That'll be Dannreuther. You'll excuse me?

ADRIANA: Naturally. [**WYNTON** *exits. Silence.*]

KATJA: Do you think he's a homosexual?

ADRIANA: Why would I think that?

KATJA: I hear he shaves his legs.

ADRIANA: That doesn't make him a homosexual.

KATJA: His chest, too.

ADRIANA: My statement still stands.

KATJA: And his testicles.

ADRIANA: He's not a homosexual. I can attest to that. [*Pause.*] Though he does wear my panties.

KATJA: No!

ADRIANA: When I let him.

KATJA: Captain Phelps! Really?

ADRIANA: I was referring to Del. [*Silence.*] He's been like a brother to me, you know, over the years. Or a cousin, perhaps. The kind of brother or cousin who teaches you things, the kind you look up to and admire. Until one day you wake up with his raw and bleeding heart in your hands. [*Pause.*] I love him. I really do. I love dear old Delbert. [*Pause.*]

I'd never eat his heart. Though he has eaten mine. [*Silence.*]

KATJA: Do you remember Parky?

ADRIANA: . . . Your doll?

KATJA: Yes.

ADRIANA: Good Lord. How could I forget him? Your cow. Your little plush cow in the light green shirt and colorful trousers.

KATJA: Parky. Parky the Cow.

ADRIANA: How you loved that doll! You took him everywhere. You spoke for him. You let him know precisely where he stood and just who was in charge.

KATJA: I loved him.

ADRIANA: Well, I loathed him. I loathed that cow. You would take it into your head to marry him. And what a loathsome creature he turned out to be! To take that hideous bullock and turn him into the cow of your dreams. Couldn't speak, couldn't stand up for himself, only had the one outfit! . . . A dumb animal. A loathsome cow-eyed cow only fit for slaughter.

KATJA: He was very good to me.

ADRIANA: With your money, yes. Certainly.

KATJA: His daddy—Daddy Cow—had something wrong with him. He shook all the time and couldn't stop . . . soiling himself. Daddy Cow had lots of money and lots of cars.

ADRIANA: A cow with cars! Can you imagine! Whatever did he do with them?

KATJA: He sold them to other cows. Daddy Cow wore a broad-brimmed hat and spoke with a drawl. Mommy Cow drank too much and slept with bulls who didn't shake all the time.

ADRIANA: Daddy Cow shook himself to death, didn't he?

KATJA: Over a period of years, yes. Eventually he lost all control of his functions. Couldn't chew his cud. Couldn't walk through the pasture. Couldn't even moo.

ADRIANA: Poor Daddy Cow . . . And then what happened?

KATJA: Parky the Cow went to school. I wrote all his papers for him.

ADRIANA: Now why would you do a thing like that?

KATJA: Well, he really wasn't very bright.

ADRIANA: He was just a cow.

KATJA: Yes. He needed all the help he could get. And I did it because he loved me. No one had ever loved me before, and no one has ever loved me like my dream-cow loved me, and I was happy.

ADRIANA: For a time.

KATJA: For a very long time. [*Pause.*]

ADRIANA: He's not the only one who loved you.

KATJA: Who else was there?

ADRIANA: Del, for one. I know Del loved you.

KATJA: Oh?

ADRIANA: He gave you that fucking cow, didn't he? [*Silence.*]

KATJA: You know who he reminds me of?

ADRIANA: Daddy Cow?

KATJA: Del.

ADRIANA: I've no idea.

KATJA: Shakespeare.

ADRIANA: And why is that?

KATJA: He may be dead, but his works live on.

ADRIANA: But Del isn't dead.

KATJA: Of course he isn't.

ADRIANA: We'd have heard something about it.

KATJA: Yes.

ADRIANA: And I've heard nothing.

KATJA: No. [*Pause.*]

ADRIANA: They're only trying to frighten us.

KATJA: Yes.

ADRIANA: That's all they're doing.

KATJA: Yes. [*Pause.*]

ADRIANA: That's all. [*Pause.*]

KATJA: Yes. [*Silence. Lights fade. Distant rumbling, increasing in darkness.*]

2.

Lights up. Rumbling fades. **ADRIANA**, *with a drink.* **WYNTON** *enters with luggage, sets it down, exits.* **KATJA** *enters with luggage, sets it down, exits.* **WYNTON** *enters with luggage, sets it down, exits.* **KATJA** *enters with luggage, sets it down, exits.* **WYNTON** *enters with luggage, sets it down, exits.* **KATJA** *enters with luggage, sets it down, exits.* **KATJA** *enters, followed by* **WYNTON**. *They exit. They enter, carrying a large trunk. They exit with trunk. They enter. Pause.*

ADRIANA: You can put all that back, you know. [*Pause.*] I'm not going.

[*Rumbling. Rumbling increases. Lights fade. Rumbling fades in darkness.*]

3.

Lights up. **ADRIANA** *and* **KATJA**, *both in coats. Silence.*

KATJA: You know you'll enjoy it, Danny. We'll be able to see Crossley and Philly and Cecil and Mavis and Yvonne whenever we please. Won't that be lovely? [*Pause.*] I think it'll be lovely. [*Pause.*] Danny, what's wrong? Why won't you talk to me?

ADRIANA: I'm furious. Can't you tell?

KATJA: Please don't be that way.

ADRIANA: Please don't tell me what way I should or shouldn't be. [*Silence.* **WYNTON** *in doorway.*]

WYNTON: Are you ladies ready?

ADRIANA: Have you eyes in your head?

WYNTON: . . . I'll see to the car. [*He exits. Silence.*]

ADRIANA: How are your levels? Have you checked?

KATJA: I'm at 24.

ADRIANA: That's clinically impossible.

KATJA: I'm still conscious.

ADRIANA: You're sure of that? [*Pause.*]

KATJA: I was down to 16 once and still on my pins.

ADRIANA: But were you conscious?

KATJA: Barely.

ADRIANA: I should think so.

KATJA: I was stumbling about, happy as a lark, smiling and humming and laughing. I sliced my thumb open. I didn't care. I just kept smiling and humming and laughing and laughing. [*Pause.*] I'm fine at the moment.

ADRIANA: I'm so happy to hear that. Because we can't all walk around smiling and humming and laughing and slicing our thumbs open all the time now, can we? [*Silence.*]

KATJA: I'll miss him . . . Del.

ADRIANA: If he's dead.

KATJA: Even if he isn't. [*Pause.*] I'll miss this house.

ADRIANA: It's the Russian in you. We are a nostalgic people. Strong but nostalgic. [*Pause.*] You favor your grandmother.

KATJA: Do I?

ADRIANA: Oh, very much.

KATJA: I like that.

ADRIANA: She'd be proud of you. [*Pause.*] There was a formidable woman. One crossed her or disobeyed her at one's peril. . . . Imagine losing not one but three homes in the course of a lifetime. I can only believe we made her final years happy ones. I have to believe that. [*Pause.*]

KATJA: I don't remember her.

ADRIANA: How could you? [*Pause.*]

KATJA: But I won't forget this house.

ADRIANA: Oh . . . fuck this house.

KATJA: . . . What?

ADRIANA: Fuck this house. Fuck this house and fuck you and fuck me and fuck Del and fuck Bitsy and fuck your little plush cow.

KATJA: Danny, please—

ADRIANA: And fuck this hideous country and fuck the fuck out of the fucking dispossessors who are taking away my fucking HOUSE!

KATJA: Please, Danny. Please don't get upset.

ADRIANA: Well, I am upset. I am very upset. Why shouldn't I be upset? Only a fucking fool wouldn't be upset!

KATJA: Let me get you something. You'll feel better. [*She pours a drink for* ADRIANA. *Rumbling.* ADRIANA *runs to the window.*

ADRIANA: Stop that! Do you hear me out there? Stop it! Stop it! Stop it! Stop it! [**KATJA** *crosses to her, gives her the drink.*]

KATJA: Drink that. Please, Danny. You'll feel better.

ADRIANA: . . . Thank you. [*She drinks.*] More, please. [**KATJA** *refills her glass.*] I'm sorry. I'm so sorry to have lost my composure like that.

KATJA: It's all right.

ADRIANA: It's not. Not really. I'm the one who's supposed to maintain the tone around here. I'm not supposed to have screaming-fuck-fits. Oh, no. That's not allowed around here. More please. [**KATJA** *refills her glass.*] What galls me about this situation is the lack of choice. If I wanted to leave, if I chose to leave—I'd leave. But to have no choice in the matter galls me. Fact is, I don't want to leave. I want to stay here where I've always been. I'm very happy here, thank you very much. Thank you very much, indeed. More, please. [**KATJA** *refills her glass.*] And where are we going, when we go? Has anyone addressed that question? No. Certainly not to my satisfaction. Into town, he says. All right, but where in town? And with whom? From this to—what? A tiny little house we share with some *soi-disant artiste* and his pack of yapping hounds? Greasy stoves and show tunes? Semen-stained sofas and dog-hair in the soup? We're not immigrants. We're émigrés. And it is here that we have settled. We have made this place our home. And I'll be damned if I'm leaving it. More, please. [**KATJA** *refills her glass.*] I'll be damned if I'll give all this up at the slightest hint of a little danger. Life is dangerous! We risk immolation when we step out the door! It's a truism! More, please. [**KATJA** *refills her glass.*] I'm going completely out on the edge of the tree. I know that. And I don't care. I am not all gentle milkiness and sweet consideration. There is within me bitter gall on this sad occasion. I go, I know not whither. I suffer now for what hath former been. 'Tis the times' plague when madmen lead the blind. More, please. [**KATJA** *refills her glass.*] O, for a muse of fire! . . . More, please.

KATJA: Perhaps you shouldn't.

ADRIANA: You dare to bandy looks with me, you rogue? More, please. And now, Goddamnit! [**KATJA** *brings her the bottle.*] Thank you. The point I'm making is this, dear Katja. The films of Federico Fellini constitute for me the deepest, most touching, most inventive work the cinema has ever produced. I bow to my two masters: Fellini and Del. Both are dead, and both live on. They will always be living presences in my life. Whereas everyone else is dead. Everyone else is dead. And nothing—nothing—will bring them back. [*She crosses toward the entrance.*]

KATJA: Danny, wait! [**ADRIANA** *exits as* **WYNTON** *enters. Pause.*]

WYNTON: . . . The car is here. [*Lights fade. Rumbling in darkness.*]

4.

Lights up. Rumbling continues. **WYNTON** *at window.* **KATJA**— *with tea tray—enters.*

WYNTON: Ah. Lovely.

KATJA: You'll let me know if it's too strong?

WYNTON: Certainly.

KATJA: Or if it's too weak. I had to make it myself. All the servants have gone.

WYNTON: I'm sure it's fine. [*The rumbling increases.* **KATJA** *pours each of them a cup of tea.* **WYNTON** *lifts the sugar tongs, then presents them to* **KATJA**. **KATJA** *takes three lumps of sugar. She hands the tongs to* **WYNTON**. *She stirs her tea.* **WYNTON** *takes two lumps. He stirs his tea.* **KATJA** *sips her tea.* **WYNTON** *sips his tea. The rumbling fades. Silence.*] How is she?

KATJA: She's asleep.

WYNTON: Just the thing for her.

KATJA: Yes. [*Silence. They drink their tea.*]

WYNTON: Where do you think you'll go? If you can't come back here?

KATJA: I hadn't thought about it. France, I suppose.

WYNTON: Where in France?

KATJA: Cap Martin. We have friends there.

WYNTON: Ah.

KATJA: But I don't know that for a certainty. It's not for me to say.

WYNTON: Ah. [*Silence. They drink their tea.*]

KATJA: Earlier you said . . . you said you saw Del's body?

WYNTON: Yes.

KATJA: Was it—was he . . . Was there a very great deal of damage?
[*Pause.* WYNTON *takes an envelope from an inside breast pocket.*]

WYNTON: These should answer any questions you have along those
lines. [*Pause. She takes the envelope. She opens it, removes a set of photographs. She slowly looks through the photographs. She puts the photographs back into the envelope. Silence. She holds out the envelope to*
WYNTON.]

KATJA: Thank you. [WYNTON *takes the envelope. He puts it into an
inside breast pocket. Silence.*] How is your tea?

WYNTON: Excellent, thanks.

KATJA: I'm glad. [*Silence.*] I'd hate to see anything happen to Danny.
She's been very good to me. Very good. [*Pause.*] Do you find it strange
that I call her Danny?

WYNTON: Should I?

KATJA: She's always insisted on being called Danny. She has a very
strong will. Whereas I have none. None at all. It was taken away from
me years ago. But I don't miss it. [*Pause.*] Someday I shall write a very

long, very learned book on that very subject. And in doing so, prove I have more will than I ever imagined.

WYNTON: I look forward to reading it.

KATJA: I look forward to writing it. I shall grow old in the service of my masterpiece. [*Silence.*] Did you know I've been married?

WYNTON: I didn't know that.

KATJA: Yes, I was. I was married for . . . two years—no, I take that back. Three years. [*Pause.*] He's dead now.

WYNTON: I'm sorry.

KATJA: It was a long time ago. But thank you. [*Pause.*] He had no will, either. Worse than that, he had no volition. A certain pale charm, that was all. A very pale charm. Most people loathed him. [*Pause.*] You see, I wasn't loved as a girl. I developed a wide-ranging set of illnesses because of this. Naturally I place the blame for this on my family. I am more sinned against than sinning in this respect. Yes, I have acted cold-ly—even heartlessly—but all my efforts have been directed toward health and integrity of the self. I'm still not entirely well. I'm due for a new cornea after Lent. But I have my hopes. Surely that's the impor-tant thing? [*Pause.*] I was the older, more experienced party in the rela-tionship. Men had used me in the past, used my body for their own sat-isfaction. Kip nearly destroyed me. I'd sit in my room at university, with a penicillin drip in my arm, playing my Spanish guitar and singing my songs of revenge. I'd been used by everyone but never loved. I'd almost given up when Parky found me. I was growing older. I was no longer a blushing young thing. I've never been a blushing young thing, actually. I've never been beautiful. Not like other girls. Not even in the flower of youth—such as it was, my shy and secretive youth blighted with illness and neurosis and damage. But when I saw him in his light green shirt and colorful trousers, and heard him speak, and saw that he needed to love as much as I needed to *be* loved—all that was past. A *coupe de foudre* on the grand scale. He wasn't graceful, he wasn't bright, he wasn't even very handsome. He was about as weak a cup of tea as could be imagined. But he listened to my songs, he admired them, and I loved his little drawings of pandas and ponies and baby whales. He loved me. And I loved him . . . for a time. [*Pause.*]

WYNTON: You loved him for a time. And then . . . [KATJA *smiles, shakes her head. Silence.*]

ADRIANA: [*Off.*] Katja? . . . Katja! . . . [ADRIANA—*in her underclothes, hair and make-up mussed—enters.*] . . . Katja—I need you . . . [*She turns and exits.* KATJA *rises.*]

KATJA: . . . Excuse me. [*She exits. Lights fade. Rumbling in darkness.*]

5.

Lights up. Rumbling continues. ADRIANA—*in robe—asleep.* KATJA *nearby.* ADRIANA *moves. Pause. She moves again.*

KATJA: . . . Danny? [ADRIANA *is still. Pause. She shudders into consciousness.*] Danny, what is it? . . . Danny?

ADRIANA: Oh Jesus . . . Oh God in Heaven . . . Oh . . . Oh . . . Oh . . .

KATJA: Danny, what is it? What is it? What's wrong?

ADRIANA: . . . Oh . . . Oh . . . Oh . . . [*She begins to cry.* KATJA *crosses to her, puts her arms around her.*]

KATJA: Danny? . . . Don't cry, Danny . . . Danny . . . What's the matter? Did you have a bad dream? . . . What's wrong? What's wrong?

ADRIANA: . . . It's happened.

KATJA: What? What's happened? . . . What's happened, darling?

ADRIANA: . . . It . . . It's happened. I saw it. It's happened. Oh God. Oh Jesus. It's happened. I saw it . . .

KATJA: You saw what? What's happened? What are you talking about, Danny? Tell me. What's happened? What did you see? What's happened? . . . Danny? . . . What? . . . [**ADRIANA** *sobs. Lights fade.*]

6.

Rumbling fades in darkness. Lights up. **ADRIANA,** *asleep. A car horn sounds.* **WYNTON** *and* **KATJA**—*with coat and purse—enter.* **WYNTON** *crosses to door.* **KATJA** *stops beside* **ADRIANA.**

WYNTON: Come along, my dear. [*Pause.*] You mustn't worry about her. I'll bring her to the Palais in the morning. [*Car horn.*] Katja—it's time to go. [**KATJA** *crosses to the door.*]

KATJA: Take good care of her, Captain. She's almost been a mother to me. [*She exits.* **WYNTON** *follows. Pause. Sound of a car pulling away. Silence.* **WYNTON** *enters.*]

WYNTON: . . . There it is, my dear. There it is in the proverbial nutshell. [*He fixes himself a drink.*] Your little girl's off to the city. But you mustn't worry about her. No. Somewhere there's a young man just waiting to sweep her off her feet. [*He lifts his glass.*] To youth. [*He drinks.*] But what's to become of us, I wonder? Where will the years to come find us? Safe and sound, or sad and sorry? I wonder. . . . And I wonder if you wonder. I wonder if you wonder if I wonder . . . It's been absolutely wonderful. All of it. [*Pause.*] Reading Gide by the seaside. . . . The crashing waves, the flecks of foam, lovely . . . the scent of hyacinth. the new moon cradled in the arms of the old. . . . You were my hyacinth girl and I was your blushing beau, resplendent in my light green shirt and colorful trousers. [*Silence. A clock chimes ten times.*] Time to go, I'm afraid. The curfew, you know. [*He crosses to* **ADRIANA.**] They'll say you died as the result of an unprovoked enemy attack. No shame in that. [*He takes out a pistol.*] But what do the dead know of shame? Shame is for the living. [*He places the barrel of the gun against* **ADRIANA***'s skull.*] I want you to know that I shall carry with me always the vision of your innocence and beauty. [*Pause. Simultaneous blackout and amplified gunshot.*]

KAWAISOO
(THE PITY
OF THINGS)

by Jason Grote

Special thanks to Kate Benson and Laramie Dennis
for their roles in the birth of this play.

CHARACTERS:

Ellie: Female, 28–38; attractive

professional woman, smart, unstable.

SETTING:

A twenty-four hour grocery store

in an affluent suburb.

TIME:

Fall, 2001, approximately 2 AM.

JASON GROTE'S work has been presented and/or developed at Soho
Rep, The Flea, The American Living Room @ HERE, The Ohio, The
Makor/Steinhardt Center, Chashama, The Brick, New York University,
Columbia University, Circle X, The Bloomington Playwrights Project,
The Neighborhood Playhouse, The NY Fringe, and The Present
Company; and in the *Brooklyn Rail, McSweeneys.net*, and the antholo-
gies *Cultural Resistance: A Reader* (Verso), *From ACT UP to the WTO*
(Verso), *Captured: A History of Film and Video on the Lower East Side*
(NYU Press), and *The Billionaires for Bush Guide to Being Really
Really Really Rich* (Four Walls Eight Windows). Honors include run-
ner-up for the 2002 Princess Grace Award. He is currently writing a
site-specific play commissioned by Sanctuary Playwrights' Theatre and
is, with Sarah Benson, a co-chair of the 2004–05 Soho Rep Writer/
Director Lab. He has an MFA from NYU and lives in Brooklyn with his
wife, writer/editor Lorraine Martindale, and their cat, Murray. He is
proud to be included in this book.

ELLIE: If we could just pause for a minute before we go in. I am . . . cogent enough to realize that my saying that this is a holy space would strike most people as odd. I realize this. But Michael, I want you to understand that this is a very difficult time. I know that sounds selfish, I mean, imagine what you must have gone through, and Courtney and Josh, and that little blond chippie of yours—

Joking, I'm joking. What I'm saying is that I have no intention of using my illness as a—

Michael, the banality of this place is exactly the quality that makes it holy. Can I—I know that this is not the appropriate time to dwell on such things, but when I first got the news—the first news, you and the slut, not this news—I came here—not for any therapeutic reason, you understand, but because we needed groceries—and found enormous comfort, enormous stability. I have grown fond of it. Sometimes I think that's why it's really open twenty-four hours, because it needs a time to be a cathedral. The housewives and the screaming kids leave and it gets to become what it truly is. Please be respectful, Michael. I know how laughable I am.

I'd like to start in aisle six. That's my favorite place, right between the Surf With Active Oxygen and the abrasive Tweety Bird heads.

Before I start the tour, I'd like to point out some general characteristics. First, the gentle hum of the fluorescents. Notice how they're not too bright, not blinding, don't make you feel like a deer. The floors: earth tones, allowing one to avoid noticing the inevitable grime that accumulates on lighter shades of linoleum. The products: all faced. That's an industry term, faced. It means they're all even, symmetrical, soothing, not strewn chaotically all over our—all over the shelves. The music:

Hall and Oates. Can't win them all, I suppose. Still, it beats orchestrated string versions of "American Woman," or an endless loop of early Whitney Houston singles.

My point, Michael, is: I am well aware of the criticisms that you and others put forth, that my perfect little world here is in fact predictable and artificial, and inescapable, that it spreads its monocultural virus throughout the world, but I hold that these critics have not paid attention to the subtle, all-important differences that class and geography provide.

When I go into the poor supermarket—the one down Route Thirty-Three, with the limited produce selections and the gray meat and the dingy floors—I start to—I can't breathe, it's so—It's horrible, I know, you would be—you must be so ashamed, I know that poor people need a place to shop too, but—well, I'm sure it's not pleasant for them, either—the no-frills products? Have you seen these? Plain white boxes with the product names stamped on? BEANS. CORN CEREAL. It makes me so sad, so acutely aware of the fragility of human life. I look at these cans and boxes and I feel like I'm watching an old woman teetering at the top of a staircase.

I need packaging. It's the faces, mostly. Happily smiling at me. Paul Newman, our savior, avatar of tolerant, pluralist American liberalism and salad dressing, so like you, except for the salad dressing. And the looks. Take heart. I hear he's had cosmetic surgery. Elmo, the Rugrats, the Keebler Elves. All the animals in the pet aisle, the ones we don't eat, staring lovingly at us, asking us why we have failed them. They don't put pictures of the animals on the meat. Imagine that? A happy little cartoon bunny glued to a gamy, plastic-wrapped carcass.

You may be pleased to know that I no longer eat animals.

I suppose we should begin the tour. You may have noticed a slight burning sensation in your mucous membranes from all of the detergent. That's why I like to start here. Awakens the senses.

On your left you'll notice a wide and colorful variety of antibacterial dishwashing liquids—a triumphant but ultimately futile gesture. Remember these: you'll notice a striking parallel once we get to the Gatorade.

To your right you will see what is probably my favorite feature: the scented candles. Many an hour have I stood here smelling these air-freshening sacraments. In fact, I have the section memorized: indulge me for a moment, won't you, Michael?

Peach Sensation, Crisp Breeze, Sunsplash, Vanilla Essence, Country Berries, Gardenia, White Bouquet, Mystical Serenity—smells like a grandmother, Honeysuckle and Pear, Lilac Spring, Waterfall, Sweet Nothings, Botanical Sachet, Hawaiian Breeze, Sensual Spice—smells like someone stuck pumpkin pie spice up his or her ass, Mountain Berry, Strawberries and Cream, French Vanilla, Mango Splash, Sensual Rose, Summer Blossoms, Tropical Melon, Relax and Refresh, Hazelnut Vanilla, Heather Mist, Soothing Sandalwood, Invigorating Lemongrass —smells like some dimly remembered infant anxiety, Romantic Jasmine.

Lately I've been working on memorizing the actual scents, so that I could identify them without looking.

Perhaps the most impressive thing is that every last one of those candles was made in the United States of America. I pay attention to that. I do. I am well aware of the concept of commodity fetishism and of Marx' labor theory of value—surprised? All this time I've had on my hands since the dust from the custody wars settled, I've been reading your old books—*Das Kapital* was a fucking doozy—

But I hold these products, Michael, and I imagine each and every hand that has labored over them, the Chinese mother of five stamping plastic knife handles out of a mechanical press, the Wisconsin woman with the hairnet and the obsolete name, like *Ethel* or *Bertha* unrolling long sheaves of aluminum foil—the twenty-year-old Mexican patriarch lugging box after box from a splintery wooden palette—all so I can have this wondrous gift of order and abundance. My relationship with them, with this place, these things—the Japanese have a word for it, kawaisoo, the pity of things. It's moved beyond fetishism for me. It's commodity love.

Sometimes it's not enough to touch the things, to smell them, buy them, or eat them. Sometimes I want to submerge myself in the clear plastic tubs of nonpareils and macadamia nuts. Sometimes I could cover myself in the cool, foam-packed meat.

But that would be crazy!

I don't know about you, but I'd like to get out of aisle six before my eyeballs start to fizz and sizzle from the fumes. Aisle seven: seems like a logical progression.

Aisle seven! A cavalcade of American obesity! On our left: row upon row of beautiful soft drinks, flirting with us from behind their veils of plastic and tin. On our right: salty snack foods engineered for maximum crunch potential. I feel the most affection for the also-ran soft drinks. It's like going to see a garage band that specializes in Foghat covers.

[*Introducing Michael to "Doctor Skipper."*] Michael, "Doctor Skipper." "Doctor Skipper," Michael. "Mountain Breeze." "Punch." Punch! Deliberately vague, that one. "Strawberry." One wonders.

Gatorade. What is it? Where does it come from? Is it antibacterial? What, exactly, makes pink juice? We shall never know.

Aisle eight: the ethnic aisle. This part reminds me of the City and therefore of you. As far as I'm concerned, the presence of this aisle renders the City irrelevant. But still. I remember our stupid little culinary adventures in places like Weehawken or Jackson Heights, squeezing like the self-congratulating, masochistic liberals we were through dusty holes-in-the wall piled high with Vitarroz crackers or tamarind paste. This aisle's—it's like that place in Barbados we went to. Grinning natives happily refilling your drink, their hostility tucked away in a tin shack somewhere, with their poverty, far away from the tourists.

Nine, baby aisle, let's skip this one. Obvious reasons. But give me a second here— [*She disappears and returns instantly, holding a package of disposable diapers.*]

A sensible precaution.

Ah! Here we go: ten. The cosmetics! An island of big promises in an ocean of little promises. In this aisle reside the secrets of eternal beauty and unconditional love. Sometimes I get in trouble for abusing the free sample privileges. What can I say? There's a cute college boy who works the checkouts before midnight.

Jealous?

The odd little hair devices—bangles, brushes, clips. I don't imagine she uses these. Or does she? Does she still have that lesbian haircut? I suppose I'll find out at the funeral.

Sometimes I look at all the people on the exotic black person hair products and imagine I'm in Harlem in the 1920s, dancing with Langston Hughes, Josephine Baker singing, I'm feeling Langston's smooth brown skin, smells of sweat, rum, and pomade.

The white people hair dye. This part's fun. A gradual rainbow of hair potential. From a distance it looks like a seamless transformation from vampire black to nutty redhead to platinum Marilyn. I love them all.

When I look at them my jealousy dissipates. I want nothing more than to touch their laughing, waxy lips.

Sometimes I like to engage in a little 1-800 action.

[*She takes a cell phone from her pocket and dials the phone number on the back of a dye box.*] Have you noticed this? Every single product here comes with eleven digits of untapped potential. Every product here comes packaged—at no extra cost—with the promise of actual human contact. Such as it is.

Hello?

Excuse me.

Yes, hello. I had a—a question.

If your hair dye—the, uh—the model on the package—

[*She doesn't really have a question. To Michael:*] Small talk can be difficult.

[*Into phone:*] The model on the package, is she actually—has she actually used the dye?

Right. Is she—uh-hum. Uh-huh. Right. So she is actually—yes.

Is she there?

Is she there. May I speak with her?

May I speak with you?

Hello?

Yes, I am—well, I—nothing, really.

I—

Where are you?

Did you know anyone?

Good. Good.

[*She starts to get choked up.*] Yes.

My ex-husband. Yes. New York.

Thank you.

You too.

[*She hangs up. Beat. She smiles. She pulls an item from the shelf.*] My favorite item. The Breath Remedy Tongue Scraper! Made in the USA by U.S. DenTek Corporation, located at 307 Excellence Way, Maryville, Tennessee. Can you picture it? Born-again Christians strolling through the manicured grounds and air-conditioned skyways of hushed corporate parks. When I hold the tongue scraper, a feeling that I can only describe as patriotism wells up in me. I am so inspired by the notion that something this absurd would be profitable enough to get itself planted in every grocery store in the United States. And it is. I always check.

Patriotism, that seems to be the thing these days, doesn't it? The flag protector spray: probably my favorite bit of nationalist hucksterism. You must just LOVE that. That must be the most FITTING fucking trib-
ute—

I'm sorry. That was hostile.

I do my best.

Ooh. This is good up here. Close your eyes. Just trust me. Close them!

Ta-dah! The produce section! The picture of American dominance, opening like the Emerald City, like the gates of heaven itself. You can drown yourself in pomegranates, in gala apples, in Asian pears. And all that work you did, all that bitching and moaning about the United Fruit Company funding nun-rapists, or whatever—isn't this all worth it? This plenty, this comfort.

Death squads have never been so delicious!

You were so proud, working there. CISPES. Pardon me if I can't share your enthusiasm. I found the counterrevolutionaries as gruesome as you did, but . . .

Well. I guess not enough for you. Or as much as she did. Or maybe it was just her tits.

[*Picks up a bunch of grapes, starts plucking them and throwing them at him.*] I hope the two of you managed to stop plenty of baby-massacres together. You fucker. [*Her heart isn't in it. She stops.*]

This was supposed to have been the our big confrontation. I've fantasized about this hundreds of times, smashing a watermelon over your head, force-feeding you grapes—are grapes okay to eat again?—over and over I tortured you with fruit, I buried you in cantaloupes, one time I even put garlic in your eyes—But you—having been reduced, I suppose, to crispy pork skins covered in melted office supplies, and, oh, thousands of tons of dust—

[*She starts throwing grapes again.*] What the fuck kind of place was that for a fucking poverty NGO anyway? You fucking asshole, you smug, do-gooder shit—poking your blond, world-saving fucking graduate student—though I guess she's out of school now—

YOU HATED THOSE WALL STREET FUCKS!

[*She takes a breath. As she speaks, she starts removing the diapers from the package and taping them to herself, making a kind of diaper armor.*] I should get ready. They were just buildings. They got to us, sure, but if—if they really want to destroy us they will come here, attack us here, where we're safe, where we store our flags and our cigarettes and our nineteen different kinds of water—our greeting cards—That would be real terror, a million planes falling into our supermarkets, paper sale signs tearing as glass windows shatter, the cheap toy machines exploding in a hail of molded plastic crap, for a split second every child's fantasy until the child realizes what just happened, what is happening. Our landscape seared forever. Imagine how that would look to God, if you believed in God? How beautiful would that be. Pop! Pop! Pop! Pop! All over America. The most accurate map of us there has ever been. [*Pause. She is now covered in diapers. She looks at the empty package.*] I guess I have to go pay for these now.

I fear the checkout. I hate to go through alone. It's so cold and ugly, closing the deal, walking through that gauntlet of impulse purchases. There's no cute college boy, either. Just a grumpy old Filipino woman who thinks I'm crazy. Pfft.

And those tabloids. Did you know, Michael, that it's always you staring out at me, through the eyes of every sordid celebrity, UFO alien, smoky satanic visage. It's you. Especially lately.

It all seems so trivial now. The jealousy, the meds, those fucking meds. Courtney and Joshua.

Since January I've looked at the collapsible child-seat basket on the grocery cart and been hit by an acute sense of how empty it is. That isn't even the best part. I'm used to that. It's that you're dead and I'm nuts and somewhere your grad student is pushing them around a store,

Courtney banging her feet against the walls of the cart, Josh standing up behind her, sticking dried cranberries in her ear. Does she yell at them? Do they even do that anymore?

I know you didn't believe in God or heaven or any of that. Wherever you are I hope it's banal and stupid and means absolutely nothing to you. It's the banality of things that makes them holy. [*She exits. End of play.*]

HIPPIE VAN GUMDROP

by Dan LeFranc

for Ryan, Kay, and Bud

CHARACTERS:

Syd

Dana

DAN LeFRANC'S plays have been produced at Actors Theatre of Louisville, Santa Cruz Actors' Theatre, and the American Theatre of Actors in New York. He is a graduate of the University of California, Santa Barbara.

Hippie Van Gumdrop premiered on February 4, 2004 at Actors Theatre of Louisville, directed by Wendy McClellan.

The back of a large old van, converted into a dingy living space. The floor is carpeted in an offensive dull hue, tie-dye cloths are nailed into the sides, CD cases are strewn about, a twin mattress rests on the floor covered with leopard-print bed sheets, a few torn bean bag chairs, a cooler, a couple plastic storage bins, oodles of random shit, etc. It appears as if it has been neglected and abandoned recently. It smells like bologna. Two young women, SYD and DANA, are picking through the atrocity. They carry cheap white trash bags. As they speak, they are examining objects and occasionally tossing them into the bags. Something about SYD suggests a teeming water balloon, DANA resembles a titanium dam. Pause.

SYD: Back in high school, when I ran away from home, I met this guy named Lightning Mike. We called him Lightning Mike because he drove this big blue van. A big blue freeway chariot, with this big ass lightning bolt running across the side of it. The guy also did a lot of speed, like a yacht-load of speed. He couldn't slow down, always on something. The van smelled like shit. Like stuck in the air Coke can crusty Funyuns shit. Every Saturday night around 2:00 AM, Mike'd pull up to Mary's house—you remember Mary, right? Bleach blond, Smurf tattoo. She's who I was staying with. God, mom flipped out. She called all my friends and they all lied to her about where I was staying even though they all knew I was staying with Mary. So mom freaked and hung posters with my second grade class photo on every lamppost for, like, twenty miles. Anyway, so Mike would pull up to Mary's and yell something like, "The milkman's come for your children!" I don't know, he did a lot of speed. We'd all pile in the van and—Mike had jet black hair all spiked up with a yellow streak running down the middle to go with the whole, you know, lightning motif. But the thing is he never put Dep or L.A. Style in it, it just always stood up. He'd try to Dep it down with a comb or blow dry it for hours, anything, and it always stood up because, uh, he did a lot of speed. So, we'd fly down Olympic or Sepulveda or whatever until we got to some shops and Mike would suddenly stop the van, leap out holding this huge ass brick and chuck it through a window. We all had bricks. But I only chucked the dark red ones. They reminded me of the handprints Mom would leave on our asses when we were kids. Remember, when we'd both run into the bathroom and pull our pants down in front of the mirror to see who had the reddest butt, or the nastiest handprint welts? You always won! [SYD *laughs,* DANA *does not.*] Man, I loved those fucking bricks. Anyway, one day, I wasn't there, I heard about it, it was over at this guy Jason's house. Mike was all fucked up, making quesadillas in the kitchen and talking to Jason when his face sorta zapped out, and suddenly he fell facedown right smack on one of the electric burners. Mike didn't even flinch when he hit the burner, and his face cooked there for almost a minute, because, um—See, the weird thing was, they had an open casket and where Mike fell on the burner, around the top of his forehead, he had this big bubbly sickle. And the mortician or whoever preps the body combed his hair down over the burn, and, it was funny because he was finally able to have his hair combed down. Lightning Mike finally had his hair down, and he looked, so, so dead. [*Pause.* DANA *examines a plastic gold broach.*]

DANA: This is all so—

SYD: So—

DANA: Shitty.

SYD: Yeah.

DANA: This is ridiculous. What are we supposed to be looking for?

SYD: Valuables.

DANA: I know, I was being—

SYD: Uh, he said, "Ladies, we're sorry about your mother, but we need to ask you to remove any valuables from the vehicle immediately."

DANA: Yeah. Valuables. Fuck you, Officer, Officer—

SYD: Gil.

DANA: Whatever. Fuck him. Fuck Officer Gil. Sounds like a molester.

SYD: He seemed *very* nice.

DANA: God.

SYD: What?

DANA: Nothing.

SYD: What?

DANA: You make friends like everyone else makes a salad. Makes me want to ram your head into a wall. [*Pause.*]

SYD: Hi.

DANA: Hi. [*Pause.*]

SYD: It's good to see you. Real good.

DANA: This is shitty.

SYD: How long's it been?

DANA: Valuables. This is all a bunch of crap. Why the hell does she have an abacus? These CDs. Whose CDs are these? Kenny Loggins, Wings, the *Moulin Rouge* soundtrack—newly inducted gay men listen to this shit. When did she start wearing orange? Orange looked terrible on her. And all this cheesy plastic gold—her wardrobe looks like a Klimt painting. None of this meant anything to her. None of it. Is this really her stuff? Look, meditation balls. She hated the Chinese. I can't tell what's hers, and what's clutter.

SYD: I miss you.

DANA: Yeah.

SYD: Hey, I miss you.

DANA: I heard.

SYD: Would you fucking talk to me?

DANA: Hey, there is a tow truck waiting outside to take this van, house, harem, whatever—

SYD: I know—

DANA: —Over to the junkyard to be crushed into a goddamn gumdrop. I didn't come here to catch-up. I didn't come here to mend old wounds, or giggle about Officer Fish Fucker's handlebar moustache. I am here to put Mom in a box. That's it. I came clean and I'm leaving clean. Nothing complicated. Nothing emotional. [*Pause.*]

SYD: I have this new boyfriend who's really into juggling. His name's Todd. He juggles all sorts of shit. Mugs, keys, fruit, dime bags. Todd keeps a glass cup full of super balls next to his bed. He'll juggle them laying on his back at night while I watch him. He never talks, but he never drops a ball. I guess it's kind of compulsive and weird and potentially homicidal, and I expect it'll get on my nerves real soon, but right now it's really really hot.

DANA: WHEN DID SHE START LISTENING TO LIL' KIM?

SYD: I thought you sent her that CD, for Christmas one year.

DANA: Huh. [*Pause.*]

SYD: When Mom came to visit you out in Nebraska. What did you say to her?

DANA: I told her I knew, and she could go rot.

SYD: Oh.

DANA: Yeah.

SYD: She was young then, she wasn't as—

DANA: Don't talk to me about young. Young has nothing to do with it. Are we keeping any of this shit?

SYD: Don't blame me.

DANA: I'm not blaming you. It doesn't matter. I just want to know what's getting squished and what we're gonna hock.

SYD: I feel lonely, Dana.

DANA: Hey, this looks like it's worth something. What do you think? Six bucks? Seven?

SYD: I feel lonely.

DANA: Mm hm. [*Beat.*]

SYD: You're, like, made up of dark matter. You're the Borg. Or, or moon ice. You don't need anything. You could live in a black hole. I'd at least need a joint. I don't do alone.

DANA: What about the juggler?

SYD: He's really good at juggling. He's a great juggler.

DANA: He can teach you how to juggle, and you can teach him how to love. Fairy tale. Boom.

SYD: It isn't enough. Anymore. With Mom now. Everything looks so big. Dialing the phone, cooking pasta, talking, juggling. Enormous. Everything takes up too much space for, uh, it doesn't leave enough room, enough time, for, uh, uh— [SYD *lightly holds* DANA's *forearm.*

DANA *tenses and becomes quiet.*]

DANA: Syd, I know you're feeling a great sense of, of, loss or something. And I'm sorry, but—Look, the woman put me up for adoption when I was four years old.

SYD: But she kept you!

DANA: She—The family who was set to adopt me had me strapped into a car seat in a station wagon with a bow in my hair. When they started to drive away, she, she screamed. She chased the car down the street, barefoot, and pounded on the windows of the car. I was only four, but I remember this flash of her face in the window: all red, a string of spit hanging out of her mouth, a piece of something black stuck in her tooth. What I really remember is the feeling. The feeling's still stuck. I remember feeling that the woman in the window—what she was feeling, what I was feeling—it wasn't love, it was absolute terror. [*A startling knock on the van.*] ALMOST FINISHED, GIL.

SYD: Dana—

DANA: I say fuck it, let's squish everything.

SYD: Dana—

DANA: We'll put the cube in the coffin with her. Very pharaoh. She can listen to Lil' Kim in the afterlife. [DANA *moves to open the door.*]

SYD: I want the CDs. [DANA *stops. Groans.*] I'm going to make a mix tape. All of Mom's favorite songs. I'm going to play it at the funeral and force everyone to listen to me sing every single one. And you'll sing with me. We'll sing together. People will cry, and, um, clap. [SYD *begins to sing.*] *Getcha getcha ya ya da da / Getcha getcha ya ya here here /* Now together. / *Mocha chocolatta ya ya /* Come on. / *Voulez-vouz coucher avec moi, ce soir? / Voulez-vouz coucher avec moi, ce soir? /* I'm not going to do it by myself.

DANA: Syd—

SYD: I have a burner. And friends with huge speakers. We'll fucking rock.

DANA: Syd, I don't have room for a sister. [*Pause.*]

SYD: You—

DANA: What? I what?

SYD: You look so ugly. [*Pause.*] Your face, it's sunken. Your eyes were never that dull. Your hair looks ratty. God, you look like M—

DANA: Don't.

SYD: I never in a hundred years thought I'd end up being the pretty one.

DANA: Yeah, well.

SYD: You know, I look up to you. Not only in that little sister engrained in my psyche sort of I look up to you way. But more real. Like the way I look up to Lance Armstrong, or Madonna.

DANA: Thanks. I look—at you—and you completely—astound me. I need to get wasted.

SYD: She, uh, must have kept some liquor in here. [**DANA** *and* **SYD** *rummage with renewed interest.*]

DANA: When she visited me in Nebraska, before she decided to discover her tantric frontier in the Mystery Machine, she stole four bottles of Albertson's scotch from my freezer.

SYD: Huh.

DANA: I watched her do it, and I let her, I think, because I was hoping she'd drink it all at the same time.

SYD: That's—a yacht-load of scotch.

DANA: I've never felt so little about something in my life. All I have is this taste stuck in the back of my mouth. I don't know even know what it tastes like. God. That's all I can muster: this fucking—taste.

SYD: Potpourri. Maybe that's what it tastes like. In the back of your mouth. I get that sometimes.

DANA: I've never tasted potpourri.

SYD: Me neither. [*A loud knock on the van.*]

DANA: HOLD ON.

SYD: Hey—? [**SYD** *has found a portion of the carpet that peels up. Wood is seen underneath the carpet.*]

DANA: What is it?

SYD: I don't know. Help me tear off this piece of wood. [**DANA** *helps* **SYD** *pull at the piece of wood, until it rips off the floor of the van, kicking up dust.* **DANA** *and* **SYD** *toss aside the wood plank and look inside the hole.* **SYD** *drops her arm in and searches.*] Huh.

DANA: What? What did you find? [**SYD**'s *face turns perplexed. She takes her arm out and looks in the hole.*]

SYD: Nothing. There's nothing in there. It's empty.

DANA: Huh. [**SYD** *and* **DANA** *stare at the hole. Knocking on the van door.* **SYD** *and* **DANA** *continue to stare at the hole, oblivious to the sound. The knocking gets louder and louder. End.*]

DEAR
SARA JANE

by Victor Lodato

CHARACTERS:

There is only Sara Jane.

VICTOR LODATO is a 2003 Guggenheim Fellow, as well as the recipient of the 2003 Weissberger Award for his play *Motherhouse*. Other plays include *The Bread of Winter, Wildlife, The Eviction,* and *Slay the Dragon*. Additional honors include a Helen Merrill Award, as well as fellowships from the National Endowment for the Arts, The Princess Grace Foundation, and The Camargo Foundation (Cassis, France).

His work has been produced at Actors Theatre of Louisville (Humana Festival), Magic Theatre, Ensemble Theatre of Cincinnati, and Mill Mountain Theatre. His plays have received workshops and readings at Manhattan Theatre Club, ACT, The Guthrie Theatre, Williamstown Theatre Festival, Primary Stages, and the O'Neill Playwrights Conference. He has received commissions from South Coast Repertory and the Magic Theatre, where his new play *3F, 4F* will be staged in 2005.

Mr. Lodato is a Phi Beta Kappa graduate of Rutgers University, and a member of New Dramatists and The Dramatists Guild of America.

Lights slowly up to reveal a young woman, seated next to a small table.
On the table rests a human skull, a letter, perhaps a framed mirror in
which the skull is reflected. As the lights come up, we see the woman in
profile, regarding the skull. A contemplative mood, reminiscent of a
Georges de la Tour painting of Mary Magdalene. The woman wears a
nightgown. It is evening. She stares and stares at the skull. Finally, she
turns to the audience. Though emotionally agitated, she attempts to
appear casual, composed—even lighthearted.

SARA JANE: I love my husband. Jerry. I love him. I do. Green eyes.
With little bits of copper in them. And his hair, his hair is this wonderful color. Cinnamon. He's a looker, Jerry. And this deep voice. It rumbles. Rumbles. Makes you melt. Just melt. And big, big beautiful hands.
And they're always warm. Mine are always cold. Ice. Even in the summer. Crazy. But him. Jerry. You'd think he was running a fever. I'm
burning up, he always says. I'm burning up. I put my feet between his
legs. At night. They get so cold. And in the winter—terrible. I put
them between his legs. Oh, and he curses. It's so funny. Says I'm gonna
give him a heart attack with those feet. But he lets me do it. He must
be sweating over there. Cause it's so hot there. Where he is. Very hot.
And I mean *hot.* I worry about him. It hardly seems real. All of this. I
don't like to watch it. On the television. I turned it on once, and there
was this picture, this, this image. Oh, I mean I just don't know about
television in general. Lowers your intelligence. And half of what you
see is probably not even true. Half at least. I'm not going to let my children watch it. Not too much anyway. Jerry and I don't have kids yet.
We're gonna have them though. Two or three. He says two. I saw this
image. Children running. And it looked like the street was a river. Of
blood. Some of the children were bleeding. Some children were drag-
ging other children. Trying to carry them. Maybe they were dead, I
don't know, you couldn't tell. And the screaming was like birds—I've
never heard screaming like that. Like a singing, like a siren. And the

street like a river. And they were running. And I kept thinking, shoes of blood. Couldn't get that out of my head. Shoes of blood. Isn't that funny? Shoes of blood, shoes of blood, shoes of blood. [*A nervous giggle.*]

I could not get that out of my head. Just spinning. Around and around.

I get so tired sometimes. Sometimes I'm walking down the street and I feel like I could just lie down, right there, on the street. You know, if I'm walking. On my way home. Or heading downtown. Going to meet someone for lunch. Maybe my mother. Last week, I saw a man on the street. Asleep against a building. Middle of the day. Wrapped up in a blanket. Not a blanket, a—a black bag, a plastic bag. Well, you see that all the time, men like that on the street. But this particular day, when I saw that one man wrapped up in that bag, I thought to myself, I could do that. Just lie down. Take a little nap. Isn't that funny? Because I was tired. You know? And what else was I going to do anyway. Go home and no one's home. Or go to some restaurant. Meet a friend for lunch. You say, *friend. Friend.* What does that even mean? And then you go to lunch. And talk about what? Talk about nothing. So why not? Lie down. If a person is tired, then a person should lie down. *Friend.* I mean isn't that a funny word? *Friend. I* after *E*, except after *C*. It's not a simple word. The end of it and all. Think about that. The *E-N-D*. There's one side, your side, and then there's them, there's the enemy. That's what this is all about. The one side, your side, and then the enemy. Some of yours die and some of theirs die. That's how it is in these situations. I read in the newspaper about this one village—it was all women and children, just like they say in the movies, you know, to make it very dramatic, women and children—and they were all killed. They were all burned. Well, you know, they say even the children are setting traps in the woods. That these children, from a very early age, are taught these things—how to set these horrible traps that can kill a man. If he walks into one. I'm not saying these children in this village were killers. I'm not saying that. Because I know I was very upset when I

read about this burning of this village. I talked to my mother about it.
Because I was confused, I was upset. But what you have to realize is
that innocent people always die in a war. That's what she said. She said:
'Honey, innocent people always die in a war, that's just the way it is. In
a war.' And that word! Is it a war, isn't it a war. Oh, my god. They don't
stop with that. A *war*. And doesn't that word get stuck in your mouth.
War. Like you've got a big piece of gum in there. Or like everything's
starting to slow down. *War. Waar. Waaar.*

Oh, Jerry. [*She looks at the skull.*]

Poor Jerry. [*She gingerly touches the skull.*]

I love my husband. I love him. I do. [*She looks at the audience.*]

Oh, no, this isn't—you didn't think this was—this isn't Jerry. This is
not my husband. Did you think that? Oh my god, isn't that funny? This
isn't Jerry. This is—this is something else.

I don't really understand the whole thing. You know? I don't get it.
This house, it's a beautiful house we live in. We've only been here six
months. It's got a sun room. They call it a sun room. There's a swing
set out back. Rusty—but Jerry says he can fix it up. He's an ace at cars.
Fixing cars. That's what he was doing. Before he left. But he's going
back to school when he comes home. He will come home. Because
we're just a couple of miles from the community college. And we don't
know what yet. He's not sure. What he's going to study. Restaurant
management, I thought. Oh, I would love to open a restaurant one day.
Jerry's not sure. Maybe hotel management, he says. But definitely management. I mean, he's got the look. And he's smart. He is. You wouldn't
think it at first. But he is. He's quick. He's funny. Oh, my god, is he
funny. Makes everybody laugh. I mean, how could a person maintain
even a basic level of sanity in the middle of all that? All that blood.
And snakes, there's snakes, you know, everywhere. And the screaming.

And explosions. Something happens to your mind. Something must have happened to Jerry's mind to do something like this. Running around in the woods. Not the woods, that's not what they call it. The jungle. The jungle? What does that mean? Am I saying that right? Jungle? Is that a word? I'm not going to pretend a person could maintain—maintain their what?—manners?—maintain their manners in the middle of something like that. In the middle of a *jungle*. In the middle of a *waaar*. Oh, you know what he could do? He could study graphic design. Because he used to be really good at drawing. When he was a kid. He showed me a couple of pieces. He really should go back into that. Into his art. He's got these big, big beautiful hands. And he's always got ideas, always got a hundred ideas. We have these stools in the basement, for the minibar, and they're all made from tires. Car tires. And, oh my god, they're so comfortable. And you should see the doodles he does on the phone pad. Animals and people and clouds and just lines and things, all swirled up into nothing particular, but really good. He's really good. [*She looks at the skull, touches the eye sockets.*]

This is where the eyes were. Here. One here. And one here. Little eyes. Slanty eyes. And there was a brain in here. And skin. All around. Tongue. Lips. Just like a regular person. Eyebrows. Hair. Ears. He did it all himself. Jerry. Cleaned it up. All of it. Yes, he did. Oh, my god. And he did a good job, didn't he? He's an ace at cars. With his hands.

I love my husband. I do. Dear Sara Jane. *Dear* Sara Jane. That's me. Sara Jane. My husband's Jerry. Jerry sent me this. Jerry sent me this skull. In a box. Jerry Housetree. I took his name. Of course I did. Sara Jane Housetree. Isn't that funny? Like a tree you could live in. Like a children's story. Jerry Housetree. My husband. Sent me this. Sometimes you just watch the light crawling across the wall. All day. The light comes in the window. And it hits the wall, then slips down, and then it crosses over to the other side, and then it's gone. You don't even see it move. It moves when you're not looking. Like a clock. Then it's gone.

And it's dark. Dear Sara Jane. [*Trembling, she picks up the letter from the table, reads.*]

Dear Sara Jane. *That's me.* I miss you, baby. I miss your body. *My body.* I miss all of you. I am thinking of you always. I want—*well, that's private, that part.* I dream about you every night. As you can see, there is something in here. I am sending it home to have for when I return. And it is for you too. Because we are winning and we will win. I did not kill him. He was already dead. When we found him I said he was mine. I took his head with my own knife. Not easy. I boiled it down, scraped it, then boiled it again. It is bleached and so it is clean, don't worry. We will keep it. It is terrible but we are winning. I will be home soon. Hi to your folks and your brother. Tell him I have something for him too. Who loves you? Do you know? Take a guess. Jerry. Jerry. And Jerry. [*She puts down the letter, her hands still shaking.*]

Do you know, on our honeymoon, we stayed in a hotel that the people in the town called *la belle du nuit.* That wasn't the real name, but it was on the top of a hill, and all lit up at night, so it looked very beautiful from down below. When you drove up to it, at night, you wanted to cry it was so—it was like a place you'd always been dreaming of. And you were going there. I mean, how do you ever really know another person? Really know them. I have secrets. Sure I do. Even from Jerry. I have dreams. I have ideas. Things you'd be embarrassed to say. But you know what? Because I've been thinking about this. When Jerry comes home, I'm gonna tell him everything. Everything. I'm not gonna be embarrassed to tell him anything. And I want him to tell me everything. I mean, my god, how could he—? Because two people should tell each other—shouldn't they?—they should tell each other every little thing. So there's nothing between them. Because doesn't it feel sometimes there's a life inside you and it's trying to come out, it's trying to find its way out. So you have to talk about these things. Where have we been? Where are we going? Because you don't want to get lost. I want to have everything in order. Everything in order. When Jerry comes home. Because that's when our life starts, doesn't it?

I just wish I could fall asleep. That's the thing. Just a few hours of sleep. Because you don't want to get lost. [*Pause.*]

And it's so quiet in the house, isn't it? Oh my god, it's so quiet. [*She looks at the skull.*]

And this one—this one—says nothing.

Who loves you? Do you know? Take a guess. Jerry. Jerry. And Jerry. [*She looks at the audience.*]

I'm so scared. I'm so scared. I'm so scared. [*Blackout. End of play.*]

CHINA

by Scott Organ

CHARACTERS:

Karen

Elizabeth

SCOTT ORGAN is from Virginia and lives in New York City. Since 2001, his one-act plays *and everybody else . . .* , *True North*, *Break Room*, *Runners,* and *The Mulligan* have appeared at the Atlantic Theater Company's 453 New Works series, a series he helped create and which he continues to produce. His play *Fixed* premiered at the Hangar Theatre in Ithaca, New York, and in Los Angeles, his play *City* premiered with Circle X Theater Company—where it earned a Drama-Logue Award for Excellence in Playwriting. Mr. Organ's full-length plays *The Faithful* and *Belly of the Whale* have had readings and workshops in New York, Los Angeles, Virginia, and Washington D.C. He is also the author of the screenplay *Ghostkeepers.*

An office. ELIZABETH, *early–mid-20s.* KAREN, *a little older, a presentation in hand.* KAREN *looks quietly at* ELIZABETH.

KAREN: How big would you say China is?

ELIZABETH: I'm sorry.

KAREN: China. How many people do you think are in China?

ELIZABETH: I don't know . . .

KAREN: Because it's 1.3 billion.

ELIZABETH: Oh. Okay.

KAREN: Do you think that this company could benefit from an association with a country like that?

ELIZABETH: Of course.

KAREN: So you think maybe adding another, I don't know, say, 500 million people to our client base would be a good thing?

ELIZABETH: Well, yeah.

KAREN: Well, then, there's this one thing I don't understand.

ELIZABETH: What's that?

KAREN: That here at the bottom of the PowerPoint presentation that you typed up, which is designed to do exactly what we were just talking about, that down here on the last slide. . . . Under benefits here. The bullet points. We've got "establish a presence in financial services industries in China." So far, so good. And then we've got "build on pre-existing private banking ties." Which makes good sense. And then we've got on the last bullet point there—"continue our pattern of world domination through suppression of the poor, widening the gap between the rich and the poor and, most importantly—the fattening of our already fat-ass wallets."

ELIZABETH: Huh.

KAREN: Yeah.

ELIZABETH: I think that's a little too candid.

KAREN: Do you? [*Pause.*]

ELIZABETH: Yes, I did that.

KAREN: I know.

ELIZABETH: I did that as a joke. Gary is supposed to, he's the . . . you know, it's his job to edit these things. I've had this bet, this ongoing bet, because you see, Mike and some of the others think that Gary has no sense of humor. But I think he must. And I wrote that in, thinking, well, it's going to be edited. Because that's what you do when you edit. You look at it.

KAREN: Gary has a sense of humor.

ELIZABETH: He does?

KAREN: He re-formatted his hard drive this morning which some might find funny.

ELIZABETH: He did?

KAREN: Right after I fired him, yes, he destroyed everything on the computer.

ELIZABETH: You fired him.

KAREN: He wasn't supposed to go back to his desk. That's how it's done these days. We have a couple security guys escort you out. But he said he'd left his allergy medicine. And then it was just a matter of typing "format c:".

ELIZABETH: You fired Gary?

KAREN: All the big companies do it this way. Call you in to a meeting, have a couple of blue-jacketed security types walk you out. Somebody else cleans out the desk, sends it to you. This way you avoid any sort of difficulties. Any sort of vengeful or embarrassing behavior.

ELIZABETH: Why did you fire him?

KAREN: You said it yourself. He's an editor. That's his job. Like you said, as an editor, you look at it. He obviously didn't look at it. That's his job.

ELIZABETH: He missed one thing. One silly little thing.

KAREN: That one little thing was copied 220 times, was sent downtown, was sent to the researchers, was sent to China. That one silly thing is in China now. It's in China. China is a huge country. [*Pause.*]

ELIZABETH: What are you going to do?

KAREN: What do you think I'm going to do?

ELIZABETH: Well. You fired Gary. And Gary didn't even start this thing. So . . .

KAREN: You flaunt the dress code, you know that?

ELIZABETH: I what?

KAREN: That Friday. Last April.

ELIZABETH: April?

KAREN: Those were blue jeans. Those jeans were blue. And blue is strictly forbidden.

ELIZABETH: What are you talking about?

KAREN: And I know what you were thinking. You were thinking they were indigo. That they were indigo. Not blue. But Elizabeth. Indigo is a sort of blue. You know that. I know that.

ELIZABETH: This was four months ago?

KAREN: And they were the low cut. They were low. It's casual Fridays, Elizabeth. Not hip-hop Fridays. Casual.

ELIZABETH: I don't remember. I'm sorry.

KAREN: And I know sometimes you don't wear a bra. [Pause.]

ELIZABETH: Excuse me.

KAREN: And no, there's nothing specifically in the dress code about that. I've done it myself if I have a thick sweater on, just as a matter of comfort. I've done that once or twice. But the way you did it was very different and no there is nothing specifically in the dress code about that but nor is there something which states the men can't wrap their penises in a sock and walk around with them hanging out. . . . [Pause.] It's common sense. You see? When you're walking down the hall, you know? All jiggly? Do you see what I'm saying?

ELIZABETH: You don't pay me to jiggle.

KAREN: That's right. And I know you're poking fun, but that's absolutely correct.

ELIZABETH: I can't believe this.

KAREN: There is a pattern of behavior here, Elizabeth. This has been going on for a long time.

ELIZABETH: What? My bralessness?

KAREN: Your insubordination. Your subversive behavior.

ELIZABETH: I'm subverting something?

KAREN: We have rules for a reason. This is the head office. This is a major institution. Just today, on page 2 of the *Financial Times*. Did you read the article? No. Of course you didn't. Why? Because you don't give a shit.

ELIZABETH: Yeah. That's right.

KAREN: You're a . . . you're a what? What are you?

ELIZABETH: I don't understand the question.

KAREN: You're a something else. You're a painter, or a sculptor, a poet. What else are you?

ELIZABETH: I dance. I dance and I sometimes play bass.

KAREN: And you think that you stand above it all because of that.

ELIZABETH: No.

KAREN: You've got some sort of dream, right? Some sort of thing that gets you through the drudgery here. You have some sort of hope. And in the interim, you're gonna subvert. With your socialistic comments, which I'm sure you don't even understand, with your flaunting of the dress code. But have you taken the time to realize that you are a part of this corporation. You are doing the work. You. Me and everyone else. And you. You. If this corporation is shredding the fabric of this world, then it is you who is doing it. Do you see that? You can make all the smart comments you want in some bar somewhere, but you're the one doing it. And just because you play bass on the weekends does not make your participation any less significant. You live, you eat, you take dance class, whatever, because of this bank. What am I going to do? What do you think I'm going to do? I'm going to do my job, which is a whole hell of a lot more than you've ever done here.

ELIZABETH: I need this job. I really need this job.

KAREN: But this job does not need you. It does not want you.

ELIZABETH: You mean you.

KAREN: I'm speaking for the company. And who do you think you are? Who do you think you are? I've been asking myself that question for a long time.

ELIZABETH: I have bills to pay.

KAREN: As does this institution.

ELIZABETH: It's very . . . do you know anyone who's looking for work? It's very hard out there.

KAREN: You should have thought of that before.

ELIZABETH: I'm two months behind on rent . . . [*Pause.*] This is personal for you.

KAREN: If caring about my job is personal then yes, I am taking it personally. [*Pause.*]

ELIZABETH: No. I know about you.

KAREN: Is that right?

ELIZABETH: Yeah. That's right. And I'm sorry if your engagement didn't work out . . .

KAREN: Who told you that?

ELIZABETH: But you've got no right to shove me around. Because some guy dumped you a week before your wedding.

KAREN: That's not. . . . That has nothing to do with anything.

ELIZABETH: No?

KAREN: It's impertinent to the. . . . And beyond that, it's untrue.

ELIZABETH: You're a cold woman. You always have been. I don't blame him. I don't blame him for dumping you like that. Dumping you, what, six days before your wedding. The little cryptic cards you sent out. The little white cards. I saw them—we all saw them. "The so and so wedding will not take place." And that's all it said. What the hell is that? You think people aren't going to figure that out?

KAREN: No, he . . .

ELIZABETH: And you see me getting along well here, you see me not living as if this fucking bank were the only thing on the planet and maybe it pisses you off. Well, Karen. It's not my fault. Not my fault your almost-husband walked out on you. It's not my fault that you've made this bank your entire world. What is my fault? I played one silly little joke. I take responsibility for that. I'm sorry. Does that mean I should be fired? I don't think so. As for everything else your accusing me of, as for the alleged blue jeans and my decision to forego a bra, I can only imagine that you are somehow jealous of me, or angry at me, or taking your bitterness out on me because of your own stupid stupid wasted life. [*Pause.*]

KAREN: Right.

ELIZABETH: I guess that's that then.

KAREN: My own stupid stupid wasted life.

ELIZABETH: I take back one of the stupids.

KAREN: No. No. [*Pause.*] He said it was because he was sick.

ELIZABETH: Who?

KAREN: My fiancé. My ex-fiancé. He said it was because he was sick. Because he's sick. He's sick, you see?

ELIZABETH: I'm sorry.

KAREN: I thought, I don't care if you're sick. I thought, I love you, Chris. I thought, I love you. And we'll get through this thing.

ELIZABETH: I'm sorry. I didn't know.

KAREN: But do you know that what he meant was he was sick in the head.

ELIZABETH: What do you mean?

KAREN: Which is what I asked him. And what he meant was that he was depressed. And I said to him, I said, so what? You're depressed. Everyone's depressed. Everyone. He couldn't marry me because he was depressed. How is that supposed to make me feel? [Pause.]

ELIZABETH: Depressed?

KAREN: Well, yes. Yes. Yes. And Elizabeth, this fucking bank is the only thing in the world. You're right about that. And do I take your behavior personally? Yes, I do. Elizabeth. I do. This bank is the only thing in the world. And I sit around thinking well if it had just been a brain tumor. Then everything would be okay. If it had just been spinal meningitis or some sort of deadly spore in his lungs or Hanta Virus or the fucking plague then everything would be so much better. What would you write on the cards? What in the fuck would you write?

ELIZABETH: No, I don't know . . .

KAREN: It's not always the war we imagine it to be. Not always the war.

ELIZABETH: What do you mean?

KAREN: In the beginning it feels like love, you know? But in the end it's just people being burned and shot and hacked up. You know?

ELIZABETH: I don't understand.

KAREN: If I had been his puke-bucket girl, you know? That has some sort of resonance. If he had been sick. But depressed? [*Pause.*] My stupid stupid life.

ELIZABETH: I didn't mean that . . .

KAREN: I want to kill you, you know that? I daydream about gutting you with a steak knife. You make a joke, you put it in the presentation. The way you walk around in those skirts. China. It's my ass we're talking about. All of China. I can't . . . [*Long pause.*] You know, there's always been this big vague thing, which is "what I want to create." This big vague thing I never understood where to put it. And I thought maybe this bank. I thought this bank. I thought China. I thought China. I thought Chris. Chris is part that thing. Or China. I kept thinking I've got something big under here somewhere. I daydream about steak knives and guns. My sister told me that those things represent my potential. Knives and guns. Because I got this big vague thing . . .

ELIZABETH: It's okay . . .

KAREN: This big vague thing that looks just like you.

ELIZABETH: No, it's okay.

KAREN: It looks just like you.

ELIZABETH: Hey. Karen. It's okay.

KAREN: It's not okay. How you can say that?

ELIZABETH: Maybe not yet. But it can be.

KAREN: Call somebody.

ELIZABETH: Who?

KAREN: Somebody bigger. Someone who can help.

ELIZABETH: Okay.

KAREN: Somebody bigger than China, if that's possible.

ELIZABETH: Yeah, okay. Don't worry. We'll call someone.

KAREN: Okay. [*Pause.*]

ELIZABETH: This is good, Karen. Good to talk. Do you feel better?

KAREN: I feel different.

ELIZABETH: But better?

KAREN: A couple things, Elizabeth.

ELIZABETH: What?

KAREN: You bring in blue-jacketed security guys why? So you have no difficulties. No vengeful or embarrassing behavior.

ELIZABETH: Right.

KAREN: Which I didn't do.

ELIZABETH: Okay.

KAREN: I didn't bring them in. You didn't even pick up on this. I'm not firing you. I'm not firing you.

ELIZABETH: No?

KAREN: No.

ELIZABETH: Why not?

KAREN: I care too much about you.

ELIZABETH: Okay.

KAREN: It's just sometimes I don't understand what to do with you. Do you know what I mean?

ELIZABETH: I think I do, yeah.

KAREN: And Elizabeth.

ELIZABETH: Yeah.

KAREN: The second thing.

ELIZABETH: What?

KAREN: I thought your thing was funny. It made me laugh. Don't dare tell anyone that.

ELIZABETH: I won't.

KAREN: But it's true. I laughed. [*The end.*]

THE
MULLIGAN
by Scott Organ

CHARACTERS:

Bill

Eddie

SCOTT ORGAN is from Virginia and lives in New York City. Since 2001, his one-act plays *and everybody else . . .* , *True North, Break Room, Runners,* and *The Mulligan* have appeared at the Atlantic Theater Company's 453 New Works series, a series he helped create and which he continues to produce. His play *Fixed* premiered at the Hangar Theatre in Ithaca, New York, and in Los Angeles, his play *City* premiered with Circle X Theater Company—where it earned a Drama-Logue Award for Excellence in Playwriting. Mr. Organ's full-length plays *The Faithful* and *Belly of the Whale* have had readings and workshops in New York, Los Angeles, Virginia, and Washington D.C. He is also the author of the screenplay *Ghostkeepers.*

A bar. A table. **BILL** *sits at the table with a beer. Nearby,* **EDDIE** *stands with a beer. They're not together. They drink.* **BILL** *sees* **EDDIE** *standing.*

BILL: Have a seat.

EDDIE: No thanks.

BILL: No. I mean it.

EDDIE: You mean it?

BILL: Yeah. You know. I'm not just saying it.

EDDIE: Thanks. Yeah. Okay. [**EDDIE** *sits.*] Dogs are barking.

BILL: What?

EDDIE: My dogs.

BILL: Oh. Okay. Right.

EDDIE: My feet.

BILL: No. I know.

EDDIE: You know?

BILL: Yeah.

EDDIE: Because you looked like you didn't.

BILL: Okay. You caught me. I didn't. I was being polite.

EDDIE: Busted.

BILL: Yep.

EDDIE: Hey. No harm, no foul.

BILL: Okay.

EDDIE: Life is hard enough as is, you know . . .

BILL: You got that right.

EDDIE: Without having to interpret some guys vernacular . . .

BILL: Yeah—I have no idea what you're talking about.

EDDIE: Hey—now that's more like it. [*Pause. They drink.*] Place is busy today.

BILL: Yep.

EDDIE: And how many people do you think are going back to work? A couple drinks for lunch and back to work.

BILL: I don't know.

EDDIE: I am. Are you?

BILL: Got the day off.

EDDIE: Not me. Not me. It's back to work. So I have a couple beers, who's the wiser?

BILL: Yeah. I don't know.

EDDIE: As long as I get my job done, right? What do you do?

BILL: I'm out of work right now.

EDDIE: Oh. Well that blows.

BILL: Yeah.

EDDIE: I been there.

BILL: It does blow. It blows.

EDDIE: No, I know. And of course you got your wife on your back, right?

BILL: How you know I'm married?

EDDIE: How do I know?

BILL: You couldn't've seen the ring . . .

EDDIE: Married men look a certain way.

BILL: They do?

EDDIE: Yes, they do. Here. What about me?

BILL: What about you?

EDDIE: Am I married you think?

BILL: I don't know. Yeah?

EDDIE: You see? Because that's absolutely correct.
We have a certain look.

BILL: What look?

EDDIE: A certain "I know my place" look. We're retired, you know.
From the game of trying to get laid. We've got the look of retired ball
players. We loved the game, had our day, but now we just sit around
with other retired ball players and talk about the good ole days. . . . And
our wives, they're kind of like the car dealership we open after retiring.
We love it, put our time into it, it is, in fact, our lives. But get a couple
beers in us, what we fantasize about is not the day we started selling
Isuzus. No. We fantasize about being back in the game. So maybe we
have to get a girl on the side, you know?

BILL: I love my wife.

EDDIE: I never said you didn't. I love mine too. That's not what I'm
saying. No, I'm sorry. It's me. I love my wife too. But love has no bear-
ing on problems, you know?

BILL: Yeah, I guess so.

EDDIE: Sure, you know, love, love, love, everybody's got that going on, but what about the bills, you know?

BILL: Yeah. I know. I know.

EDDIE: Sure. I absolutely love my wife. But that doesn't necessarily make things easier.

BILL: No, you're right.

EDDIE: It's hard no matter what.

BILL: You got that right.

EDDIE: Love don't pay the bills.

BILL: Yes, I've noticed that.

EDDIE: My wife, God bless her, she, uhh, you know—you do what you gotta do at work. I work a lot.

BILL: Yeah?

EDDIE: And she does, too. But I guess I work all the time. And I lost a lot of money in the stock market, you know?

BILL: Yeah, I never had that problem.

EDDIE: They say if you can't afford to lose it, don't put it in. But, you know, I thought I was gonna get rich. But, then again, I'm not the sharpest knife in the drawer when it comes to money. What's your name?

BILL: Bill.

EDDIE: Mine's Eddie. I lost a lot of money, Bill. So I work a lot. You know, and my wife is cheating on me . . .

BILL: I'm sorry.

EDDIE: Yeah.

BILL: You know this for a fact?

EDDIE: Yeah. She doesn't know I know. But I do. An interesting thing, Bill.

BILL: Yeah?

EDDIE: All the evidence is there.

BILL: What do you mean?

EDDIE: The little crimes people commit. An affair. Whatever. People wear that shit like a neon sign on their foreheads. It's just that most of us prefer the safety of delusion, so we just don't see it. But it's right smack there in front of us. It's just too painful to acknowledge. So most of us choose not to see it. But it's there.

BILL: Well. I'm sorry.

EDDIE: Ah, you know. . . . I work hard at my job, I like it, I like to do well at it, and also so my wife and I can be secure, you know? And I guess she gets lonely and starts banging the physics teacher at the school where she works. Life's funny that way.

BILL: Yeah, it is.

EDDIE: A guy just tries to do the right thing.

BILL: Yeah, no. That's true.

EDDIE: But, uh, sometimes, what is the right thing, you know?

BILL: No. I know.

EDDIE: Life is frickin' funny like that. Cracks me up sometimes.

BILL: I been out of work for six months.

EDDIE: No shit?

BILL: Yeah. My wife still has her job, she's a secretary. But I was the one who made most of the money.

EDDIE: Six months. Jesus. So meanwhile your self esteem is taking a pounding.

BILL: Yeah, it is.

EDDIE: And, you know, "what happened to the guy she fell in love with?"

BILL: Yeah, that's right. She's asking that . . .

EDDIE: You're asking . . .

BILL: Right. Right. "Where is that guy?"

EDDIE: And it gets so big. "Am I still in love", "did we just fail", all that shit.

BILL: And our house burned down.

EDDIE: It did?

BILL: Yeah. It burned to the ground. Everything burned down.

EDDIE: I'm sorry.

BILL: And how are you supposed to maintain a marriage when you begin to feel that you're just this piece of shit. And who deserves who? And then if you're not careful it gets to "I just need somebody to pay me some attention." You know? And who's to blame? Anybody?

EDDIE: My wife and the physics teacher. She did the deed, you know. But I guess I opened the door.

BILL: Well . . .

EDDIE: No, you're right. We need to be responsible.

BILL: I don't want to lose my wife.

EDDIE: Of course you don't. You would do just about anything to prevent it, wouldn't you?

BILL: That's right. I would.

EDDIE: No. I don't want to lose my wife either.

BILL: Of course.

EDDIE: Don't you wish life had time outs?

BILL: Yeah.

EDDIE: You know, "time out, folks." Everybody freezes or something. You take a nap, gather your chi or something. Whatever.

BILL: Would be nice.

EDDIE: Or if life had mulligans.

BILL: Mulligans?

EDDIE: You know, in golf. You get to replay one hit.

BILL: Oh.

EDDIE: You know, "hey folks, I call do-over."

BILL: Yeah.

EDDIE: You fuck up the project at work. Or you didn't try hard enough to get that girl's number six years ago. You know?

BILL: I wouldn't mind that.

EDDIE: But you're not drinking your days away, are you?

BILL: Oh, no. No. I'm, uh, I've got this meeting with the insurance company. No. I just had to get out of the motel. And I'm early for the meeting. So I came here.

EDDIE: That's good. The booze is not gonna do the trick.

BILL: No. I go out. I look for work. And, uh, it's not as easy as it used to be.

EDDIE: No. I guess not.

BILL: My wife and I. We don't talk.

EDDIE: No?

BILL: No. I think we both want to, but we don't. Isn't that bizarre?

EDDIE: I don't know.

BILL: In the same room there. At nights. For hours.

EDDIE: Doesn't sound like things are too good right now.

BILL: No. No, they're not.

EDDIE: I'm sorry.

BILL: Yeah, they're not so good.

EDDIE: A mulligan would be nice right about now, wouldn't it?

BILL: Yeah, it would.

EDDIE: What would it be?

BILL: What would I do over?

EDDIE: Yeah.

BILL: I don't know.

EDDIE: Because remember what I was saying before, and you've got this big blinking neon sign on your forehead.

BILL: I do?

EDDIE: Yeah, you do.

BILL: You can see that?

EDDIE: Yeah, I can. I can see it.

BILL: I guess I do.

EDDIE: Hey, man. You're a good guy. I can see that about you. I can see that about people.

BILL: You see that about me?

EDDIE: Yeah, I do.

BILL: Because I'm not. Not really, Eddie. Not really.

EDDIE: You can be a good guy, partner, and still do the occasional bad thing. It doesn't take it all away.

BILL: It doesn't?

EDDIE: No way, man. No way. There's bigger things which persevere.

BILL: No. I don't know, man. I don't know.

EDDIE: I'm telling you what's true.

BILL: Laura just, uh, won't look at me.

EDDIE: Uh-huh.

BILL: I never thought my life would go this way.

EDDIE: No. We never do.

BILL: I love her.

EDDIE: I know you do.

BILL: And I talked her into it.

EDDIE: You talked her into it?

BILL: I did, yeah. I did. I thought we could start over.

EDDIE: Uh-huh. What did you do?

BILL: What did I do?

EDDIE: Yeah. What was it?

BILL: Are you a cop?

EDDIE: No.

BILL: I can't say.

EDDIE: But I know you want to. I know you do. I see it plain as day.

BILL: You do?

EDDIE: Plain as day, my friend. We all want to confess. We do. Why?
To feel better. To start again. To be straight with the world. And here I
am. Here I am. A couple of strangers in a fern bar. And you stand in
your kitchen there, and there's a little quiet part of you that just wants
to talk to your wife. But you don't. Why? And you sit here with me.
And you want to tell me something. But you don't. Why? Because the
whole world will change once again. The whole world will change. And
that's terrifying. But let me ask you something, Bill . . .

BILL: What?

EDDIE: Do you want the world to stay the same any longer? Do you? [*Pause.*]

BILL: I burned my house down.

EDDIE: You burned your house down?

BILL: That's right.

EDDIE: Why did you do that?

BILL: I took my grandfather's gun collection out—a few other things of value. I took them out of the house. It's all insured.

EDDIE: For the money.

BILL: The money? No. For my wife. For us. So I don't have to feel like the sack of shit that I do . . .

EDDIE: Okay. Okay.

BILL: Okay?

EDDIE: You're not a sack of shit.

BILL: No?

EDDIE: No. Do you feel better?

BILL: I don't know.

EDDIE: You will.

BILL: I will?

EDDIE: I guarantee it. You take my word on that. Maybe not today. Maybe not in two months, but you will.

BILL: How is it you knew I had something eating me up like that?

EDDIE: Like I said, I can just see these things.

BILL: But you're not a cop.

EDDIE: No.

BILL: What are you?

EDDIE: I'm an insurance fraud investigator.

BILL: You're an insurance fraud investigator.

EDDIE: Yeah. [*Pause.*]

BILL: Where?

EDDIE: Eastern. Across the street. I work for Eastern. [*Long pause.*]
I'm just doing my job, Bill.

BILL: Fuck you.

EDDIE: You asked me to sit down. You asked me. I'm here on lunch.
I'm having a beer and you invite me over.

BILL: Fuck you, man.

EDDIE: I wasn't trying to trick you.

BILL: No?

EDDIE: No. I was trying to help you.

BILL: You're trying to help me?

EDDIE: That's right. I can see what it is people need, you know?
Like I said. I saw you, Bill. And you wanted to talk. You needed to.

BILL: You're enjoying this.

EDDIE: No. No, I'm not. I don't enjoy busting you. Some people, yeah.
Not you.

BILL: Not me?

EDDIE: You know, there's very few reasons why people decide to break the rules like this. And all of them fall under the auspices of "money" of course. People do it for drugs, people do it for the girl they got on the side. And there's the rare person who does it for his family, you know. It's all the same crime, of course, but . . .

BILL: What are you going to do?

EDDIE: I'm going to do my job. I'm going to do my job. The wife is banging Mr. Physics, the least I could do, is do my job, don't you think? [*Pause.*] Yeah. I don't think you're a sack of shit. [*Pause.*] This is what you wanted, Bill. You made this. And it'll be better in the long run . . .

BILL: You asked me about my one do-over?

EDDIE: Yeah?

BILL: Maybe I wanted to talk to you. Maybe you're right.

EDDIE: I am right.

BILL: My wife.

EDDIE: What about her?

BILL: She would be my one do-over. She would be it.

EDDIE: What do you mean?

BILL: I wouldn't have told you that I had talked to her about burning the house down. That would be it.

EDDIE: That would be your mulligan?

BILL: That's right. [*Pause.*]

EDDIE: I come home late at night, Bill. And Mary, she's asleep there. But she'll wake up for a few moments, say hi to me, ask me about my day. Every night. Why does she do that?

BILL: I don't know.

EDDIE: Why even bother? Is it just the fear of ending a marriage?

BILL: Maybe it's just that she still loves you.

EDDIE: Yeah. Maybe. Maybe that's what it is. [*Pause.*] You got your mulligan, Bill.

BILL: Thanks.

EDDIE: Is it time for our meeting?

BILL: No. Another twenty minutes. [**BILL** *looks to* **EDDIE,** *catches the joke* . . .]

EDDIE: Okay. What do you say? Should we have another round?

BILL: Sure. Yeah.

EDDIE: All right. This one's on me.

HOPE
(AND CHARLES)

by David Schulner

CHARACTERS:

Charles: Jewish guy, late 20s

Hope: Asian-American, late 20s

Hasid: Polish guy, late 20s

Chinese Bride: Chinese girl, late 20s

DAVID SCHULNER'S plays include *This Thing of Darkness* (written with Craig Lucas; Atlantic Theater), *An Infinite Ache* (Long Wharf Theatre, Old Globe Theatre), *Isaac* (Sundance), and *Disturbed by the Wind* (New York Stage and Film). Mr. Schulner has been commissioned by The Joseph Papp Public Theater, South Coast Repertory, Actors Theatre of Louisville Humana Festival, and ASK Theater Projects. Current projects include *Ishmael* and *5*, developed at South Coast Rep and The Public Theater, respectively. His writing for television includes the critically acclaimed dramas *Once and Again* and *Everwood. An Infinite Ache* and *This Thing of Darkness* are published by Dramatists Play Service.

CHARLES *sits at a small table in a coffee shop. He is reading. Or trying to read. Or trying to look like he's reading. On another part of the stage a young* HASID *appears. He is dressed in traditional black. Wisps of a beard. He is reading. Or trying to read. Or trying to look like he's reading.* HOPE *enters.* CHARLES *does not see her. She looks at him for a moment. A young* CHINESE BRIDE *appears. She is dressed in an ornate traditional red wedding dress. She looks at the* HASID. HOPE *takes a deep breath. The* CHINESE BRIDE *takes a deep breath.* CHARLES *looks up and sees* HOPE. *The* HASID *looks up and sees the* CHINESE BRIDE. HOPE *goes to* CHARLES. *The* CHINESE BRIDE *and the* HASID *don't really move.*

HOPE: Hi. [CHARLES *gets up.*]

CHARLES: Hi.

HOPE: Don't get up.

CHARLES: I was—okay. [*They both sit down. Short pause.* CHARLES *laughs.*] Hi.

HOPE: [*Laughing.*] Hi. [*They hug awkwardly across the table.*]

CHARLES: How are you?

HOPE: Exhausted.

CHARLES: Me too.

HOPE: Did you get any sleep?

CHARLES: No. You?

HOPE: No.

CHARLES: You should have stayed the night. [*Short pause.*] Or . . .

HOPE: Did you have any . . . coffee yet?

CHARLES: [*Over.*] No. I was waiting for you.

HOPE: [*Over.*] Good. Thanks. I'll get us some. Regular? Mocha? Espresso? [**HOPE** *gets up.* **CHARLES** *gets up. The* **HASID** *gets up. The* **CHINESE BRIDE** *gets up.*]

CHARLES: [*Over.*] Regular's fine. Here, let me give you some mo—

HOPE: [*Over.*] Please don't worry about it.

CHARLES: Okay.

HOPE: I'll be right back. [**HOPE** *exits. The* **CHINESE BRIDE** *exits.* **CHARLES** *and the* **HASID** *remain standing. Then they realize they are standing alone and they sit down. They both try to read. Unsuccessfully. Then they both seem to be muttering to themselves. The* **HASID** *davens with his body as if he might be reciting a prayer.* **CHARLES** *similarly rocks back and forth but only because he's neurotic.* **HOPE** *appears with two jumbo coffee mugs. The* **CHINESE BRIDE** *appears with an elaborate tea service on a tray. Both men stop immediately.* **HOPE** *brings the coffee to the table and sits. The* **CHINESE BRIDE** *moves very slowly towards the* **HASID**. *She kind of hobbles more than walks.*]
I put in a little cream and a little sugar I didn't know how you liked it.

CHARLES: [*Over.*] That's fine. [*The* **CHINESE BRIDE** *is still hobbling towards the* **HASID.**]
I had a wonderful time last night.

HOPE: Me too.

CHARLES: You're not just saying that?

HOPE: No. I did.

CHARLES: Sorry if I was . . . awkward, it's—

HOPE: [*Over.*] Don't apologize. It was lovely.

CHARLES: Lovely. Wow. I feel like calling my mom. [*Pause. The* CHI-NESE BRIDE *finally made it. She pours the* HASID *a cup of tea.*]

HOPE: Why?

CHARLES: Oh. To . . . tell her I was lovely. My name's Charles. [HOPE *laughs.*]

HOPE: I remember. Please.

CHARLES: Okay. I wasn't sure. I remembered you're Hope but I didn't want to presume— [HOPE *is still laughing.*]

HOPE: [*Over.*] You're so . . .

CHARLES: [*Amused.*] What? [CHARLES *drinks his coffee. It's strong.* CHARLES *makes a face. The* HASID *drinks his tea. He spits it out all over the* CHINESE BRIDE.]

CHARLES: Strong coffee.

HOPE: You're different.

CHARLES: I'm different? [HOPE *nods.*] I'm not. But thanks. [*The* CHINESE BRIDE *wipes herself off. The* HASID *stands and gives her a handkerchief.*] You look good in red.

HOPE: I don't. But thanks.

CHARLES: So do you think we should date now? Or . . . [*Both couples stop.* HOPE *puts her hand on* CHARLES' *hand. The* CHINESE BRIDE *reaches for the* HASID *but the* HASID *flinches. She does not touch him.*] Was that a good silence or a bad silence?

HOPE: Was the question should we date, or would we like to date?

CHARLES: Second one.

HOPE: I mean traditionally we <u>should</u> be put to death, or at least . . . get married. [*Beat.*]

CHARLES: Are you traditional?

HOPE: No.

CHARLES: God I just saw my entire life flash by. Beheadings and weddings . . .

HOPE: But I guess we can date.

CHARLES: But not if you don't want to.

HOPE: Oh, no I do.

CHARLES: Okay.

HOPE: Okay.

CHARLES: Cool. So were kind of like boyfriend girlfriend now.

HOPE: Cool. [*Pause. They smile. They drink their coffee. The* **HASID** *takes a saucer from the tray and throws it on the floor smashing it to pieces. He smiles the biggest smile at the* **CHINESE BRIDE***. His arms extended wide in an embrace. The* **CHINESE BRIDE** *is now terrified. She kneels down to him. The* **HASID** *quickly lifts her up. They are very close now. Their arms around each other.*] We need to thank Jill.

CHARLES: Our shadchan.

HOPE: Our what?

CHARLES: It's Yiddish or maybe it's Hebrew it's one of those Jewish— it's a matchmaker.

HOPE: Oh, okay.

CHARLES: One of those meddling little old ladies.

HOPE: Right.

CHARLES: I have a shadchan story do you want to hear it?

HOPE: Sure. [*The* HASID *tries to kiss the* CHINESE BRIDE *but she breaks from their embrace.*]

CHARLES: Okay. A young Hasid—black coat black—

HOPE: [*Over.*] I know what a Hasid is.

CHARLES: Oh. Yeah.

HOPE: [*Over.*] I live off Melrose.

CHARLES: Sorry. So a young Hasid sees his bride for the very first time. She's a total . . . dog. And he's like mortified. He's fuming now. He grabs the shadchan who was trying to slip out of the room and he says, "You said her teeth were like pearls, her eyes like stars, her breasts like watermelons—

HOPE: Watermelons?

CHARLES: I guess . . . some guys like . . . that. [*The* CHINESE BRIDE *takes off a shoe and lifts her gnarled bound foot for the* HASID *to see. The* HASID *is totally repulsed.*] SO. The Hasid whispers fiercely to the shadchan, "But in fact her teeth are like rotten stumps, her eyes like muddy pools and she's flat-chested!" "No need to whisper," says the shadchen, "she's totally deaf." [*The* HASID *takes off his hat letting his long side curls tumble down. The* CHINESE BRIDE *is equally repulsed.*] My grandma told me that.

HOPE: That's good. My grandmother used to tell me all kinds of stories. Chinese legends I guess. The only one I remember is the one that—do you want to hear it?

CHARLES: Sure. [*The* CHINESE BRIDE *puts her hair up for the* HASID. HOPE *puts her hair up.*]

HOPE: When every child is young, the Gods tie an invisible red string over the ankles of the couple who will wed later in life. As the years go by, the string becomes shorter and shorter until the couple is finally united. Nothing in this world can sever this string. Not distance. Not circumstance. Not even love.

CHARLES: Beshert.

HOPE: What?

CHARLES: It's Yiddish. It's uh . . . it's the word for that story. In Yiddish. A love that was meant to be. Beshert.

HOPE: Beshert.

CHARLES: Good.

HOPE: I'm not even wearing make-up how can you stand looking at me. [*The* CHINESE BRIDE *dips her finger into the tea. She runs her finger over her lips.*]

CHARLES: Stop. You look . . .

HOPE: Don't.

CHARLES: So really really beautiful. [HOPE *laughs.*] I'm not a poet.

HOPE: Let me put on some lipstick. [*The* CHINESE BRIDE *takes a sheet of red paper off the tray and puts it to her lips. She brings the paper down. Her lips are now as red as her dress.* HOPE *puts on red lipstick.*]

Wouldn't it be funny if we both had that red string around our ankles? I mean, I'm not saying we do—

CHARLES: [*Over.*] No. I know. Just . . . what if.

HOPE: Yeah. Someone like me.

CHARLES: And me.

HOPE: And we met . . .

CHARLES: How we met. [*Short pause.*] I've never done that before.

HOPE: I have. [*The* CHINESE BRIDE *opens a red umbrella above her head.*]

CHARLES: You have?

HOPE: I used to be a bad girl.

CHARLES: Oh.

HOPE: But I'm not anymore. Until last night. With you.

CHARLES: Oh. Okay. [*The* HASID *takes his handkerchief and puts it on the head of the* CHINESE BRIDE. *She looks a little confused.*]

HOPE: You had that effect on me.

CHARLES: Had?

HOPE: Have. [HOPE *and* CHARLES *smile at each other. The* CHINESE BRIDE *and the* HASID *check to see that no one is looking. Both couples kiss. Slowly. Softly. They stop. Smile.*] And me being Chinese?

CHARLES: Non-issue. And me being Jewish?

HOPE: This is L.A.. [*Both couples kiss again. Loud shouting in Cantonese from off stage right. Loud wailing and crying in Yiddish from off stage left. The* **HASID** *and the* **CHINESE BRIDE** *are terrified. They don't know which way they should run. The shouts and cries increase. They each take off in the opposite direction. They stop and run back to each other. They hold each other for dear life.* **HOPE** *and* **CHARLES** *finish their kiss. They smile.*]

CHARLES: People are looking.

HOPE: No they're not.

CHARLES: You're right. They're not. This is so easy. [*They smile. Drink coffee. The* **CHINESE BRIDE** *and the* **HASID** *are now praying and crying for their lives as the sounds get worse.*
The end.]

THE SLEEPERS

A short play by
Christopher Shinn

for David Greenspan

CHARACTERS:

Silas

Deane

Barbara

SETTING:

A bare stage, the actors seated throughout.

CHRISTOPHER SHINN is the author of *The Coming World*, *Where Do We Live*, *What Didn't Happen*, *Other People*, and *Four*.

". . . the sick-gray faces of onanists . . ."

—WALT WHITMAN, "The Sleepers"

BARBARA: Silas hasn't kissed since Hector; Deane hasn't come since his father got sick.

SILAS: Hi. Do you want to masturbate with me?

DEANE: Sure.

BARBARA: Silas—he's the first one who spoke—and Deane—he's the second—walk to the back room of the bar they're in and begin masturbating themselves together. As they masturbate themselves together Silas begins a conversation.

SILAS: What's your name?

DEANE: Deane.

SILAS: I'm Silas.

DEANE: Silas.

SILAS: Deane.

DEANE: What's up?

SILAS: Nice dick.

DEANE: Thanks.

SILAS: Do you shoot far?

DEANE: Do I shoot far?

SILAS: I won't be able to tell, it's so dark in here.

DEANE: It depends.

SILAS: It depends?

DEANE: It depends on—you know, the last time, how close to the last time—has a lot of time passed—you know—how—you know—how turned on I am—

SILAS: Are you turned on now?

DEANE: Yeah . . .

SILAS: A lot?

DEANE: Sure—I guess—sure.

SILAS: You're nice.

DEANE: Thanks.

SILAS: Great grip.

DEANE: Sorry?

SILAS: Great grip, I like that grip.

DEANE: Oh, thanks.

SILAS: When's the last time?

DEANE: What?

SILAS: That you came?

DEANE: Um—a while.

SILAS: How long?

DEANE: Just—a while.

SILAS: Tell me.

DEANE: Shhhh.

BARBARA: They masturbate themselves together. Deane is close to coming. Silas isn't even thinking about coming. He is imagining never coming again, how marvelous it would be to masturbate endlessly, never coming. Deane begins to think about his audition on Monday morning, for a Fox pilot; then he thinks of his father, who is dying, who is in a hospital room hooked up to a chemo drip and has a few months or a year, nobody's sure. For a while both Silas and Deane are silent. In the corner a few people watch Silas and Deane masturbating themselves together and masturbate themselves. In another corner a few people watch the people watching Silas and Deane masturbating themselves together masturbate themselves and masturbate themselves.

SILAS: I'm a compulsive.

DEANE: Sorry?

SILAS: Compulsive masturbator.

DEANE: Oh.

SILAS: Three, four times a day. Even when I have a boyfriend.

DEANE: Oh.

SILAS: Do you have a boyfriend?

DEANE: No. Do you?

SILAS: No. How often?

DEANE: What?

SILAS: How often do you masturbate?

DEANE: Oh—it depends.

SILAS: Yeah?

DEANE: Yeah.

SILAS: Depends on what?

DEANE: Shhhh.

SILAS: Do you ever eat your own cum?

DEANE: Excuse me?

SILAS: Do you come here often?

DEANE: No.

SILAS: Why not?

DEANE: I don't know. I'd like to come now.

SILAS: No, not yet.

DEANE: I have a lot to do—

SILAS: Not yet.

BARBARA: They masturbate. Deane starts to get queasy, feels panic sneaking up—everywhere he looks, another crotch, another hand, another pair of eyes—balls and butts and all their smells, it's just too much! He closes his eyes, imagines his bed, safe and empty. He puts his dick in his pants.

SILAS: Did you come?

DEANE: No—I have an audition I should prepare for.

BARBARA: Then, suddenly, Deane's cell phone rings: a programmed ring: Dad from the hospital. Deane silences the phone, puts it away, and takes his dick back out of his pants.

SILAS: Change your mind?

DEANE: Did you parents ever catch you?

SILAS: Catch me what?

DEANE: Catch you—you know.

SILAS: No, did yours?

DEANE: Once, my Dad.

SILAS: He did?

DEANE: He came in, saw, shut the door and said, "Dinner's ready."

SILAS: Oh, God, you had to go have dinner in front of him—

BARBARA: As they masturbate they talk about being teenagers and masturbating—being gay and suicidal—having suicidal thoughts one minute then masturbating the next—sometimes having suicidal thoughts while masturbating—the discussion turns too serious and they stop speaking and continue to masturbate themselves together. A man with a flashlight enters the backroom, a man whose job is to make sure no one is having unsafe sex. A beam of light crosses Deane's crotch and Silas catches a better glimpse of his penis. He is struck by the shape of it, the slope, how much it looks like Hector's penis.

SILAS: Do you want to go back to my place?

BARBARA: Deane checks his phone: the voicemail icon flashes.

DEANE: Sure.

BARBARA: As they walk to the building, Silas and Deane chat.

SILAS: Britney. Definitely Britney.

DEANE: Better than Christina? Really?

SILAS: Oh come on! Britney is the new Madonna.

DEANE: Madonna was much better though, I think.

SILAS: I don't think Madonna was better, it was just a different era, you can't compare the two.

DEANE: I guess you're right.

BARBARA: They walk up to the walk up, Silas trying not to show he's short of breath. Immediately he moves towards his bathroom.

SILAS: Just gonna wash my hands.

BARBARA: In the bathroom, Silas catches his breath. Deane sits down in the living room. He notices a credenza against one wall, a month old TV guide atop it, and to the side of the credenza, a pair of black Nike sandals. Silas emerges from the bathroom, and suddenly Deane is struck by the great fragility of the human soul.

SILAS: Now, in here, I can see you how far you shoot.

BARBARA: Deane rises, passing the credenza, the month old *TV Guide*, the black Nike sandals, to kiss Silas.

SILAS: No.

DEANE: No?

SILAS: No kissing.

DEANE: Oh.

BARBARA: Silas begins to masturbate. Suddenly Deane has an image of his father, masturbating in the middle of the night in his hospital room, just after the nurse comes in to take his temperature—his father knowing he now has fifteen minutes of privacy, his weak, liver-spotted hand winding its way through the chaos of tubes, the catheter in his chest, to his penis. Deane's penis goes soft.

DEANE: Can I use your bathroom?

SILAS: Sure.

BARBARA: Deane goes to the bathroom. Silas thinks about Hector. He hasn't kissed since Hector left. Hector was eating his ass one day and was gone the next. That's love for you, no sense to be made of it. Better to keep your mouth to yourself—the mouth that eats ass, the mouth that kisses. What was it they said in Silas's high school creative writing class? Every story has a beginning, middle, and end: get hard, jerk off, and come. A kiss begins, but a kiss has no ending.

SILAS: You okay in there?

BARBARA: In the bathroom, Deane tries to get hard. It's not happening. He'll just go home. It's okay. He goes back into the living room.

DEANE: What do you do for a living?

BARBARA: Deane meant to say, "I'm gonna go," but it came out as "What do you do for a living?"

SILAS: Oh—I'm a magazine writer.

DEANE: Cool. What are you working on now?

SILAS: Um—a piece about crackers.

DEANE: Crackers?

SILAS: For Martha Stewart Living.

DEANE: Oh.

SILAS: What to put on crackers—you know—things you wouldn't normally think of to put on crackers that are good on crackers—

DEANE: Like what?

SILAS: Um—cottage cheese . . .

DEANE: Cottage cheese?

SILAS: On an herbed cracker—yeah.

DEANE: Wow.

BARBARA: An awkward silence. Time passes. Isn't that what we all need? Time to pass? But time's unforgiving: it passes when we don't wish it to, it doesn't when we do. For a creative writing assignment Silas once began a story with the sentence, "Days: we move through them, in one." He never got past that first line. It's easier to write about crackers. No one cares about moving through the days, he thought; who cares? I mean who really cares? Art, who cares? Feelings, who cares? Crackers. That was something people cared about—crackers—what to put on crackers—what to put on crackers that you wouldn't normally think of to put on crackers.

SILAS: Do you want to jerk off, or? . . .

DEANE: No, yeah, I . . . just . . . got distracted . . .

BARBARA: Silas arouses himself and begins to masturbate. Deane doesn't want to hurt his feelings—better to just come and then go. Deane looks at him, wills an erection, and begins to masturbate. They masturbate for some time, sitting next to each other on the couch, near the credenza.

SILAS: I'm close. Are you close?

BARBARA: He's not. He's far, far away, back in his bedroom, hand in his shorts, picturing Victor Hickey, soccer cleats, parachute pants, dirty knees, bloody nose. The bedroom door opens—Dad!—A gasp!—The door slamming shut!—Dinner's ready!

SILAS: Are you close?

BARBARA: Deane's hand falls away. His eyes close. He falls asleep.

SILAS: Huh? Hello? Hello?

BARBARA: Deane doesn't stir. Silas's penis goes soft.

SILAS: Wake up. Hel—

BARBARA: Suddenly sleep sweeps over Silas—

SILAS: —lo . . .

BARBARA: Silas and Deane sleep.

SILAS: [*In sleep.*] Hector . . .

DEANE: [*In sleep.*] Wha? . . .

SILAS: Camping in Vermont . . . Antique shops . . . nature . . . granola in the morning . . . Sounds . . . I wake up . . . middle of the night . . . hear sounds . . . in our tent . . . breathing . . . I look . . . Hector . . . We had sex twice that day . . . Why does he need more? . . . Playing with himself . . .

DEANE: Wha? . . .

SILAS: I wait. . . . till he comes. Then I put my hand on his chest. He gasps . . . I take my hand, covered with his cum . . . smear it on my cheek . . . look him in the eyes and say, "Kiss me, Hector." And he kisses me . . . on the cheek . . . his cum on his lips . . . "Lick your lips. Now you know how you taste. Now you know why I love you. Now you can sleep." Then he leaves . . .

DEANE: Oh . . .

BARBARA: Shhh. Their dreams have intertwined.

DEANE: Oh . . .

SILAS: Wha? . . .

DEANE: I'm in love . . . crossing the country with my boyfriend . . . going to my father, who's dying . . . We get to the house . . . I say to my boyfriend, "I'm scared to go in." And my boyfriend says, "Why?" and I say, "I don't know what to say to him." My boyfriend says, "Just tell him you love him. That's all you can do." We go inside. I call out, "Dad?" "Dad?" The whole house is dark, the blinds are closed. There's no sounds.

BARBARA: Silas's sleeping penis slowly starts to fill with blood.

DEANE: We walk to the room—the room where my father sleeps. Open the door—dark. My boyfriend says, "Open the blinds." I do. Bright light . . . See my father, asleep in bed.

BARBARA: Deane's penis hardens.

DEANE: I go to my Dad, touch his arm. It's cold. "Oh my God. He's dead." And I turn to my boyfriend . . . I turn to you—but you're not there. Search the house, calling for you. I go back to my father's room. Dad? Blinds are down again. Room's dark. Go to the bed . . . but the bed's empty . . .

SILAS: Where? . . .

DEANE: Gone . . . Lay down . . .

SILAS: Where'd I go?

DEANE: Call your name . . .

BARBARA: Silas and Deane awaken. They kiss, and as they kiss—

SILAS: Oh God.

DEANE: Oh.

SILAS: Oh God! Oh God!

DEANE: Oh! Oh!

BARBARA: —they come together.

DEANE: Oh . . .

SILAS: Oh God . . .

DEANE: Oh . . .

SILAS: Oh God . . .

BARBARA: Time passes. They drift.

SILAS: . . . what's your name again? . . .

DEANE: Deane . . .

SILAS: I'm Silas . . .

DEANE: Silas . . .

SILAS: Deane, will you wake me up in the morning?

DEANE: Sure.

SILAS: Will you be here when I wake up?

DEANE: If I wake you up in the morning, that would mean that I would be here, right? . . .

SILAS: No . . .

DEANE: No?

SILAS: No . . . you could wake me up by leaving . . . I would hear you leaving, I'd wake up and see you walking out the door . . .

DEANE: I won't do that . . .

SILAS: Promise?

DEANE: Promise . . .

SILAS: I . . . love you . . .

DEANE: I love you too . . .

BARBARA: Is there anything more beautiful than a pair of sleepers? If only they could both wake up, to see themselves asleep in each other's arms: dreaming each other's dreams, dreaming each other's need away . . . Do I have to tell you how this story ends? That in the morning, Silas awakens to find Deane is gone? But let's not end there. Let's end now—before morning comes . . . [BARBARA *looks at* SILAS *and* DEANE. DEANE *snores loudly. End of play.*]

SALVAGE
BAAS

A play in one act
by Brian Silberman

CHARACTERS:

Moses Bobo

Goody Aboo

SETTING:

The rear of "Bra Gig's Salvage Land," positioned in an open space at the edge of a rural village in Nigeria, near the town road. Mid-July 1997. Early morning. The crumpled and charred carcass of a Chrysler convertible sits on blocks in the back lot of a dilapidated and dusty salvage yard. Used auto parts, empty and rusted oil drums, and worn tires are strewn about the circle of open, dry earth and weeds. The morning's haze has yet to be burned off by the sun; the stillness of dawn yet to have been broken.

BRIAN SILBERMAN'S plays include *Manifest* (recipient of the 1998 Clauder Prize and the 2003 Pinter Review Prize for Drama), *The Yip, Throw, Sugar Down Billie Hoak, Feral Music, Half Court, Walkin' Backward, Retrenchment,* and *The Gospel According to Toots Pope.* Selections from both *Half Court* and *Sugar Down Billie Hoak* appear in Smith & Kraus's *Best Stage Scenes of 1995, Best Men's Monologues of 1995,* and *Best Women's Monologues of 1995. Walkin' Backward* appears in the anthology *Best American Short Plays of 2000–2001,* published by Applause Books. *Manifest* is published by The University of Tampa Press. He currently lives in Virginia, where he teaches in the MFA Creative Writing Program at Old Dominion University.

Salvage Baas received its world premiere on May 8, 2002 at The Ensemble Studio Theatre in New York City. The production was directed by Seret Scott.

This town will see a transformation . . .

A motor road will pass this spot.

And bring the city ways to us . . .

The ruler shall ride cars, not horses . . .

We'll burn the forest, cut the trees . . .

We must be modern with the rest

Or live forgotten by the world . . .

        —WOLE SOYINKA, "The Lion and the Jewel"

And Bongi, we can speak English—Ismasdat lapetelez for you? And I can say—Was da meta be you? [*Stops and thinks.*] Bongi, you can also have a car! Unginike ilift sihambe sobabili sigqoke kahle abantu basibuke bathi . . . hish mame, qhaks baby. Then we can go anywhere together!   —GCINA MHLOPHE, *Have You Seen Zandile?*

MOSES BOBO *and* GOODY ABOO, *men in their late forties, in the back lot of "Bra Gig's Salvage Land," seated in and underneath the carcass of an old Chrysler convertible. The car's hood has been removed, as has the front windshield and most of the engine. These parts lay in piles on the ground. The crumpled rear of the car appears to have received a blow, the obvious result of a severe traffic accident; the whole car a bit charred even, as if it were once aflame. A transistor radio sits perched precariously on the dashboard, the tinny beat of "city" music, a jiving amalgam of semi-tribal drumbeats and new, electronic rhythms.* BOBO, *only his legs visible, has wormed his way up into the engine compartment from underneath, working wrenches and pry bars on the engine support struts.* GOODY ABOO, *seated in the driver's seat, holds a lit marijuana cigarette in one hand and quietly sings a tribal song in opposition to the radio. Every so often, over the course of the play, he suffers a brief epileptic convulsion, lasting only a second or two, which neither he nor* BOBO *take much notice of.*

GOODY ABOO: [*Singing.*] "*Osee Asibe* throws away, throws away, throws away, throws away to the remotest corner. *Osee Asibe*, Child of *Adu Gyamfi Twere, Tweneboa Adu Ampafrako*, child of the Ancient God, dress up as new and let us go. Dress up as if we are new and let us go. *Osee Asibe* throws away, throws away, throws away, throws away to the remotest corner." [*There is a slight pause. He shakes his head in tired disgust and turns off the radio.* **BOBO** *calls up from the engine compartment.*]

BOBO: Eh, so! Turn the music back. [**GOODY ABOO** *does not respond.*] Eh, so. The music! [*There is a pause.* **GOODY ABOO** *takes a long look at the car and the surroundings.*] Goody Aboo!

GOODY ABOO: If it's whatever you make of it, eh Moses Bobo. Been thinking it over 'cause a' *Baas Piet* dying. That the wreckage for the one man is for the other a treasure. Eh. And who's to say it then? In the finish. To make a judgment. Eh, good. You *come.* What you *find.* In a place like this. This salvaging place. And if the treasure you salvage cannot be that thing all see as the treasure. Could it not *be*, man Bobo. Could it not be possible that a private treasure, that treasure which only oneself knows the value, is not *more* the precious. [*Loosely indicating the salvage yard and the car.*] Eh Bobo? Car like this. Could say it was a fockin' piece of Americana and you could be right. Could say with a Chrysler motorcar like this, with the first Chrysler car they built in Africa, *Baas Piet* was driving himself around a piece of something like the American Dream in Africa or something. That him sittin' up here steering around was him involved in something was bigger than himself. That this car means something. Represents, eh, something *else* than what it is. [**BOBO**'*s hand appears from the engine compartment.*]

BOBO: Hole 'n socket tool, Goody Aboo. Eh, come on. [**GOODY ABOO**, *continuing, hands over a tool from a pile on the seat beside him,* **BOBO**'*s hand taking it and disappearing back down.*]

GOODY ABOO: That if a man wants to call it the symbol for a new Africa. Calling it himself too. Ain't that right, man Bobo? A nation. 'N if he travels where it takes him. *Baas Piet* does. 'N he's got it by the reins drivin' around or whatever, so. Like he owns it. Like he's in charge. Eh? The very first Chrysler car made here. Couldn't ya say that, eh now? And that it being back in the salvage yard now as it is, eh. Do we not have the obligation. To drive. To steer. [*He stops. There is a long pause. He peers over the dash and down at* **BOBO**.] Eh man. The fock're ya after again in there? [**BOBO***'s hand appears with one of the support struts.*]

BOBO: Put this. [**GOODY ABOO** *takes the strut, turning it over in his hands. He studies it. The hand remains visible, raised and growing impatient.*]

GOODY ABOO: If a man says to himself: "I am sick of this life, eh. For I see what I am, and—

BOBO: Wrench tool.

GOODY ABOO: "And my lot too, eh. Where I am planted. Of this too. I want to move forward. To something else. To the new." So, eh. Then he'd need something. A mode of transport. To take him. To move him.

BOBO: You helpin' man or what? [**GOODY ABOO** *hands another tool over and the hand disappears again.*]

GOODY ABOO: Yeah, Bobo. Eh, Yeah.

BOBO: Don't have all day, man. Be startin' over there. [**BOBO***'s hand appears again.*]

GOODY ABOO: Eh so. [**GOODY ABOO**, *still studying the strut, hands* **BOBO** *the marijuana cigarette this time and it disappears too down into the engine compartment.*] We'll be missing the burying service. Sad about that. You sad too, man Bobo? [**BOBO** *begins to sing loudly, as he* *puffs on the cigarette, interspersing the lyrics with revving engine noises made in his throat.*]

BOBO: [*Singing.*] "Now! Smoke, quickly you have come undulating in and balled yourself up in my chest, eh. *Vroom!* Now! Fire, quickly you have just come inside and compressed yourself in a mass. *Rrrrrrrr!* Starting the engine up." [**GOODY ABOO** *joins in the song, taking up the response.*]

GOODY ABOO: [*Singing.*] "To make the road seem short, eh. To make the road seem short."

BOBO: [*Singing.*] "Now! Smoke, quickly have you come undulating in and balled yourself up in my chest, eh. Starting up the machine. Rrrrrrr!"

GOODY ABOO: [*Singing.*] "To make the road seem short, eh. To make the road seem short."

BOBO: [*Singing.*] "Now! Fire, quickly you have just come inside and compressed yourself in a mass. *Vroom!*"

GOODY ABOO: [*Singing.*] "To make the road seem short, eh."

BOBO: [*Singing*] "Now! Engine, quickly, you have just come inside to help me go! *Dayi! Rrrrr!*" [*He makes the sound of a roaring car speeding quickly, then crashing into a ball of fire and smoke, but then begins coughing and hacking from the marijuana.*]

GOODY ABOO: [*Singing.*] "Making our road seem short, eh! Now! Making this road seem short!" [*There is a slight pause, the song finished.* **BOBO***'s coughing fit subsides.*]

BOBO: Goody Aboo's fockin' stick. No sadness around when it is there too, eh so? See? Where you get it from?

GOODY ABOO: Grown from my patch. In my own soil from the village. I keep it in a pot. I have a pot of soil I took from the village. That is why it is so strong. The village. The village.

BOBO: Like an engine, eh. S'good. S'good, eh, and strong fire petrol for the engine in my chest. Make a man crash it go so fast. Make him breathe like a crashing of an motorcar it does, eh. Get his heart beating like a drum going "oom, oom, hnnnnh!"

GOODY ABOO: Eh, so.

BOBO: A drumbeat from the old village, eh. [**GOODY ABOO** *beats on his chest, as if it were the skin of a drum.*]

GOODY ABOO: "Oom, oom, hnnnh!" This is our drum, Bobo Moses. This is the talking *dundun* drum and you are holding the drumstick. It is all we have left for a drum, eh so? It is the morning and all we have left for the waking up, it is all we have to wake the Clock-bird each morning, so.

BOBO: Hey, Clock-bird! You can wake him up, Goody Aboo.

GOODY ABOO: [*Singing and beating his chest in rhythm.*] "*Kokoyinka Asamoa*, the Clock-bird, how do we greet you? We greet you with '*Anyaado.*' We hail you as the Drummer's child, the Drummer's child sleeps and awakes with the dawn, eh. I am learning, let me succeed." [*He continues the beat on his chest, encouraging* **BOBO** *to join in.*] Eh, so, Bobo. You have the stick. You have the *dundun* stick in your hand, so. [**BOBO***'s voice is heard from the engine compartment, singing.*]

BOBO: [*Singing.*] "Drum stick of *ofema* wood, curved drum stick . . . Drum stick of *ofema* wood, if you have been away, I am calling you; they say come. I am learning, let me succeed." [**GOODY ABOO** *stops the beat on his chest. There is a slight pause.*]

GOODY ABOO: I'm also sad there is no real drum anymore, Bobo Moses. Sadness for two things today. [*There is a long pause.* **BOBO** *strains to pry the remaining engine support strut loose from the car, grunting loudly from the effort.* **GOODY ABOO** *looks at the piece of support strut in his hand.*] This little piece. Here this little piece keeps up the whole engine, eh? Holds up the whole engine powers *Baas Piet*'s white American Dream in Africa.

BOBO: So.

GOODY ABOO: Don't look like it could no. Too small. [*He looks at the pile of parts pirated from the car, appraising them.*] *Bra Gig* lettin' you take this all here, eh?

BOBO: Know I want it.

GOODY ABOO: Ain't the same thing no.

BOBO: Is to me. [*A puff of smoke rises from the engine block as* **BOBO** *exhales another drag on the marijuana stick.*]

GOODY ABOO: S'why we sneakin' in, man Bobo? When they are all at the burying of *Baas Piet? Bra Gig* don't know it.

BOBO: You want to go to the burying, go to the burying then and don't help.

GOODY ABOO: Was thinking. Don't insurance need to see no? 'Fore it all gets pirated out? So *Bra Gig* can—

BOBO: Aay, fock do you care? This Chrysler car yours from America?

GOODY ABOO: No.

BOBO: You *Bra Gig* and own this salvage yard?

GOODY ABOO: No.

BOBO: Then shut the fock up then. [**BOBO***'s hand appears again, the joint in two fingers.* **GOODY ABOO** *takes it and the hand disappears.*]

GOODY ABOO: Figure for insurance papers and like so. That's all.

BOBO: Eh, so.

GOODY ABOO: 'Cause I'm betting *Baas Piet* kept then insurance papers on this fine Chrysler car way he worked on it. Got it back t'a life again . . . way this car meant to him. It bein' the Dream from America and that.

BOBO: *Baas Piet* don't gonna be needing America dreams no more. Is he? Or then insurance papers on it either no. [**BOBO** *appears from the engine compartment, climbing out with the second support strut clutched in one hand.*] 'Cause there's nothin' left of him 'round to collect on it, eh. He inna ground now here. He not studying on America's dreams, he studying dirt from the village.

GOODY ABOO: Eh, so. Think they already got him in the ground over there?

BOBO: It being his first drive in the car too, eh. It being the bust 'a cherry voyage out, eh, after salvage working. I bet insurance ain't even coming out to look here no. Jus' sign off. Not come out from the fancy town to the village. Hear about something bad as what happened t'a ol' *Baas Piet* jus' figure write off the whole thing.

GOODY ABOO: But you figure he did have that insurance, eh? Man like *Baas Piet*. Knew the value. Worth on some kind'a Americana freedom in a Chrysler. Figure he'd wanna have insurance paper on a car does what this one can. In case. In case.

BOBO: Aay fock, man, car's thing that killed him, eh. 'N that means then it's fancy Americana freedom did him in too. Know that, eh?

Fockin' freedom then give him the whiplash. Snapped his neck fine as shit. 'N after all the sacrifice he did getting it from the scrapyard. After all the sweat he dropped scraping out the rust and getting it re-chromed, eh. Fine white paint he put on. Greased up it all good.

GOODY ABOO: Eh, so.

BOBO: Turned on him. What I got t'a wait on insurance for? They killed him too. Whole lot killed him. [*There is a slight pause.*] Eh, so. Gonna finish with the helping? [**GOODY ABOO** *does not respond.*] What the fock ya come with me for then, man? What the fock you missing the burying service? Gonna say that?

GOODY ABOO: I could afford it I'd have some, eh so. Insurance. *Baas Piet* was right. *Baas Piet* knew.

BOBO: I'll tell ya 'bout insurance for a likes of you, Goody Aboo. Man like you never going to see insurance. No village man ever will.

GOODY ABOO: Aay, but if I were *Baas Piet* in a time 'a the tragedy befalling me. What I would be spending with the money from insurance! What I would be spending!

BOBO: Careful what you're wishing for Goody Aboo. What good's the insurance man's money to *Baas Piet* now?

GOODY ABOO: But I can still wish it. I can still wish it inside.

BOBO: No, I'll have no wishing here now.

GOODY ABOO: Aay, so.

BOBO: A man grown weary of trying to understand his life went into the forest, Goody Aboo, went into the forest to rest and think. [*He mimes walking a great distance and thinking hard.*] After many walking for a long time he sat down underneath a tree in the shade.

GOODY ABOO: Aay, so. Tell it, Bobo Moses.

BOBO: "How quiet," he thinks to himself, "this is such a fine lovely place. It would be so nice to live here. I wish I had a house in this place."

GOODY ABOO: Telling me a story, man Bobo? Giving me a lesson, eh?

BOBO: Says, "I wish right here I had a house."

GOODY ABOO: Okay, man. Tell me. [**BOBO** *begins to act out his story more intently, taking the role of the man sitting underneath the tree.*]

BOBO: And because this man had no idea that the tree under he had seated himself was the Wishing Tree, he was—

GOODY ABOO: Aay, Wishing Tree, Bobo Moses!

BOBO: Shut up, man. You don't interrupt my story, 'cause the man, he is amazed when this grand beautiful house rise up all around him.

GOODY ABOO: Aay, man, Wishing Tree! Tell it! Tell it, man!

BOBO: And so, "What a beautiful house," the man, he thinks, "What a perfect house I have. How happy I would be if only I was not alone. I wish I had a wonderful lady to be my companion." [**GOODY ABOO** *begins to play out the story as well; encouraged and inspired by* **BOBO***'s performance, he suddenly appears as the woman.*] And the lady who sat beside him then, man, was loving and tender and beautiful.

GOODY ABOO: Aay, man, so!

BOBO: The man embraced her, and loving her, wanted to treat her well. "I wish we had something to eat," he thinks.

GOODY ABOO: Aay, Bobo Moses! [**GOODY ABOO** *leaps up to become the food bearers, miming walking while balancing the heavy trays of food and drink.*]

BOBO: The coming of servants with food was instant, man. The food plenty and tasting and still steaming. [GOODY ABOO *sees the vision of the food and salivates, eating heartily, grabbing mouthfuls with his hands and laughing.*]

GOODY ABOO: Aay, Bobo, a wishing tree, I understand it.

BOBO: But as the man is eating he began to worry. "When I first came here," he thinks, "none of this was here. No house, no lady who loved me, no food. What is this place? Is this an evil place? Is there a demon here?"

GOODY ABOO: Eh, man. The demon, Moses Bobo. Is there the demon there, man.

BOBO: The man thinking, "What is this place? Is it evil here no? Is there the demon?"

GOODY ABOO: Aay, man Bobo! He's thinking, thinking!

BOBO: Thinking so!

GOODY ABOO: Tell it, man, so! Tell it! [BOBO *roars up as the demon, dancing and pounding his feet.*]

BOBO: And so of course the demon is fierce and horrible, wild and on fire, standing in front of the man, shrieking at him. [GOODY ABOO *cowers in fear.*]

GOODY ABOO: Aay, man! Aay, the demon standing!

BOBO: "Oh he's focking going to eat me," thinks the man.

GOODY ABOO: Aay, no thinking that! No thinking so!

BOBO: "Oh, this demon! He's going to eat me up!"

GOODY ABOO: I think he's so! I think he's so!

BOBO: "He's going to eat me," thinking this man.

GOODY ABOO: Aay, I'm thinking this! I'm thinking this!

BOBO: And the demon, Goody Aboo, eh. The demon ate him. [BOBO, *as the demon, swallows* GOODY ABOO, *engulfing him.*]

GOODY ABOO: Didn't mean to thinking that! Didn't mean to thinking that no! [*The story finished,* BOBO *steps away from* GOODY ABOO, *both of them laughing. There is a slight pause.*]

BOBO: Hear that, Goody Aboo, with your wishing and jealousy, so.

GOODY ABOO: But *Baas Piet* wasn't thinking about no demon. Man like that, who went to the white colleges in America, isn't thinking so 'bout a demon. He was driving, eh. He was going and driving, so. [*He pauses slightly, growing momentarily maudlin and shaking his head.*] Been to their schools, Bobo, and then come back to his village. If he had been here when everything happened . . . if he had been . . . Then we would not have had our trouble with these cars. Tragic. Aay, poor *Baas Piet* and the sorrowful tragic in this car.

BOBO: Ain't that fockin' tragic, eh. *Baas Piet* could see out'a that left and gimpy eye of his he wouldn't a took that intersection like he did.

GOODY ABOO: Maybe he took it that way on account of all that Americana freedom dreaming he was steering . . .

BOBO: Aay, man, no.

GOODY ABOO: How do you know, Bobo Moses? Took it on account 'a that insurance papers he was carrying too. Trusted it. Let it lead him, eh. Give himself over.

BOBO: Talking out'a your rearside now. Talking foolish.

GOODY ABOO: Eh, so.

BOBO: [*Shaking his head in disgust.*] Letting it lead him. [*He begins to clean some of the engine pieces with a wired brush and solvent.*] These parts and this engine can still be good, Goody Aboo. And I could use them to make a motorcar for me. For us. That is why I am here. Because *Baas Piet* would not mind. That is why we are missing the burying service. Okay?

GOODY ABOO: Maybe he has a doubt, eh. To know what it can amount to, him prepared for at any moment to meet with a tragical circumstance. Wants to know. What it is he's salvaged and pulled from the ground. Wants everyone to know. A private treasure is worthless to him, Bobo. It's not enough. Has to make it Americana Dream come true in Africa. Has to get it recognized. So what does he do? Insurance! Puts a price. What it's worth to somebody. What his investment in Americana freedom and in his life can add up to in a number. So he lets go 'a the wheel, eh man. Takes his hands off to see what happens.

BOBO: Nothin' like that 'bout *Baas Piet*, eh so.

GOODY ABOO: I was worth enough I'd buy insurance like no tomorrow. Aay, I'd have some already I didn't want to see the low price I'd add up to. [*There is a pause.* **BOBO** *continues cleaning the parts, dipping them into the bucket of solvent, then scraping away the rust and soot with the brush.* **GOODY ABOO** *becomes fixated on the car's steering wheel.*] Hey, Bobo, eh. Think you could get this steering wheel off for me?

BOBO: What you do with it, eh? They ain't let you drive nothing.

GOODY ABOO: I want it, so.

BOBO: Fockin' seize up. Fockin' shakes and seizures on you from the beatings, man. Look so. Ain't give no spastic a license t'a operate on the city roads.

GOODY ABOO: If it's from the beatings you ought'a have 'em too, so. How come you ain't seizing up with the shakings all the time?

BOBO: Don't know. Got a different constitution maybe. Resist the sickness they beat on us.

GOODY ABOO: It's a city sickness. It's an outside sickness. And know how I know? 'Cause it won't balance out. Eh, right? [BOBO *gets the cigarette and takes a long drag.*] The village elder cure for a sore throat. What the villagers used to do. Over where it's sore inside, you rub the outside 'til that hurts too. You rub raw all over the outside 'a where the inside hurts. Make it balance, so. Balance is the cure on those peoples of the villages. But that don't work for city pain. Maybe for the old way's kind it does, but not for the kind'a soreness now I got inside me. I tried it. It doesn't. [*There is a long pause.*]

BOBO: Aay the beatings, man. Sorry for that. Sorry for getting you those beatings.

GOODY ABOO: Eh, so.

BOBO: But what else was there but to strike? The village land for the American factory, so . . . and what else could we do, Goody Aboo? What else could we do but stand up?

GOODY ABOO: Eh, so. But if *Baas Piet* were here then . . . if he could speak for the village—

BOBO: Will be us making the cars. They tell me this. Will be us making Chryslers in the factory here if I sell them the land in trust. Laboring for city wages. Prosperity and roads for the village. *Shareholders*, Goody Aboo. The village for shareholding in Chrysler cars. This is the bargain. This is what I agreed.

GOODY ABOO: They lie man Bobo. Even Chrysler of America lies to you. *Baas Piet* would have known how they do.

BOBO: Eh, so.

GOODY ABOO: We could have waited for him to come back home.

BOBO: Fockin' *Baas Piet*, so. [*There is a pause.*]

GOODY ABOO: But you did fight them after, Bobo Moses. Fought them hard after they moved us to the shanties to build on our ground.

BOBO: Sold away the village for shareholding in their factory that we never received.

GOODY ABOO: Then you were a true leader. Then you did not try to betray us.

BOBO: It was never trying.

GOODY ABOO: "Striking!" you call out, Bobo Moses. "We are striking Chrysler!"

BOBO: It was never trying so. [**GOODY ABOO** *leaps up on the dashboard of the car, turning on the transistor radio, which emits a tinny, though throbbing, local rhythm. He turns the volume to high.*]

GOODY ABOO: Stand up in the factory and call out, "You hear that music, city people . . . Chrysler from America? You hear what it is calling? We want our shares! We are clapping our hands, we are moving our feet!"

BOBO: I brought the village music to the factory.

GOODY ABOO: "Give us the shares or we will shake things apart! We will clap and dance and our rhythm will shake you apart!" [*He begins clapping and dancing on the battered carcass of the car, as if trying to shake it apart with his intensifying rhythms and joyous movements.*]

BOBO: Eh, so, Goody Aboo! I am striking against the factory! Stop your working! Stop making the Chrysler cars! [**BOBO** *joins in the dancing,* *leaping up on the car to address the imagined factory bosses and workers.*]

GOODY ABOO: "We will bring your machines and metal down into the earth with our feet and our music! We will pound it back into where you have mined it up from our land!"

BOBO: Dancing in strike! Dancing in strike!

GOODY ABOO: "Do you hear it? Do you hear? Give us the shares! Give us what was in the bargain!"

BOBO: Clapping our hands! Moving our feet!

GOODY ABOO: "Our music still plays through your radios! Even it cannot be co-opted, eh! You still do not control it! Look! See what it does! Shake things apart! Shake things apart!"

BOBO: Village music! It will save us! It will make us right! [*Still dancing,* **GOODY ABOO** *begins to see imaginary policemen and militia approaching.*]

GOODY ABOO: And so they come, Bobo. The militia men.

BOBO: Eh, so! [*Continuing their defiant dancing, they enact their own beating at the hands of the militia, their movements more frenetic and wild, flailing their arms and writhing in a pain that is both real and imagined.*]

GOODY ABOO: Beating with sticks.

BOBO: Aay, in the face!

GOODY ABOO: Aay, in the chest!

BOBO: Dance and sing louder! It keeps them away!

GOODY ABOO: We are clapping our hands!

BOBO: We are moving our feet!

GOODY ABOO: Aay, in the head.

BOBO: Dance and sing!

GOODY ABOO: We are clapping our hands and dancing our feet, but *Aay!*

BOBO: Aay, we are dancing, eh so!

GOODY ABOO: They're hurting, Bobo Moses!

BOBO: Music! Music!

GOODY ABOO: Aay, No! [*He grabs the transistor radio from the dashboard.*] Aay, no! Blood, Bobo! All around there is blood!

BOBO: Louder! Make it louder! [GOODY ABOO *turns the volume on high, both men dancing harder.*]

GOODY ABOO: It does nothing!

BOBO: We must keep dancing! We must keep up the music to shake things apart!

GOODY ABOO: Aay! They are beating me!

BOBO: The music will protect us, the village music will keep us safe!

GOODY ABOO: No, the music is no good! It is not working! Aay, in the head! Aay, in the face!

BOBO: Dancing for the shares! Singing for the shares!

GOODY ABOO: It is too late! It no longer works! It is too late, we have sold it away to the city and now we are finished!

BOBO: Village music! Village music!

GOODY ABOO: Our music is no good, they have trapped it in a box, they have taken it in this box and it is no longer ours! I hate it! It does not sound like us anymore. It is the metal of the city, it is the concrete of their roads, it is the noises of their machines! [**GOODY ABOOO** *suddenly hurls the transistor radio to the ground, shattering it. In the silence that follows, save only for their grunts and strains as they enact the events, dancing as if their lives depended on it, they are beaten to the ground and stillness. There is a long pause. Both men lie still, recovering their breath. Finally,* **BOBO** *sits up.*]

BOBO: I got greedy, Goody Aboo. I sat under the Wishing Tree of Chrysler American and began to wishing for myself riches and new ways. New cars and roads. Shiny metal and fancy paint. I got greedy and forgot that the old ways were there. I forgot *Baas Piet* went away to learn how to help us exist in the new Africa. [*There is a slight pause.*]

GOODY ABOO: And now the old ways have gone away. Now we are without any way at all. *Baas Piet* is dead and now we are in the scrapping yard. Now we are with *Bra Gig* in the salvaging. You are no longer the waiting head of the village. No more.

BOBO: Because who will believe me, eh? Who will think that I did not sell the village to make only myself wealthy? That I did not betray them all to be like the white man.

GOODY ABOO: Eh, so.

BOBO: Even you, Goody Aboo, even you think so.

GOODY ABOO: It's powerful magic, Bobo Moses, that is in their Chryslers, that is in their factories and the cities they bring us. They have music that drowns out ours. You need an education like *Baas Piet*'s to be able to sing it and ours together. [*There is a slight pause.*] That is why I am missing the burying service. That. To say this to you. So you will know.

BOBO: Fock, you think I wanna pirate parts off *Baas Piet*'s old motor-car? Work everything off with a pry 'n a wrench? Aay, it's like I'm living in this focking salvaging yard. Like it's all I can fockin' see. Like it's all there is to this country now.

GOODY ABOO: Eh, so.

BOBO: I am building a fockin' car from out'a this. See? And I ain't taking time t'a make it cherry new like *Baas Piet* neither. Fock's the point? Only tryin' t'a hide ya started with salvage. Pretend you're something new. No. I'm gonna make mine a pirate ship, Goody Aboo, eh. And then I'm gonna drive away for the rest of my life. Know that? Get out 'a salvaging. Drive. Just drive the fock out'a here 'n t'a some place there ain't nothing to salvage. We got 'em here, ya know. Places like that. Place where something gets used up, it's used up. Ain't no little, rusted piece of it hanging on. I'm tired 'a that. I'm tired 'a just being a little, worn-out piece hanging on t'a what used t'a be something. [*There is a slight pause.*] You want t'a come with me? Please, Goody Aboo, eh. Come. I need you. Be pirates. Eh? Eh so? Burying service be over by now and *Bra Gig* be comin' back. [*There is a slight pause.*]

GOODY ABOO: *Baas Piet.* He has it figured out maybe. He thinks so, man Bobo. And then there's the *intersection.* Those roads crossing. Comes to it. He can take whichever one. Looking for the new Africa. Puts the top down. Stands up on the seat. Gets the clearest view. [*He goes to the car and stands up on the seat, looking out.*] Treasure. This intersection. That treasure which only oneself knows the value. He looks. But they're the same. All these roads. Where you are is where you're heading. 'N now he can't tell where's he's even been. Like he never moved in the first place. [*He pauses slightly, slowly getting down from the seat and sitting behind the wheel.*] What if that's what this moment was? Eh, Bobo? What would a man *think*. A man who spent his life restoring a motorcar into something to get him out, to move things forward. He thinks himself a fool, eh. He thinks himself worthless. "I wasted my life and my efforts. I dreamed the wrong dream." [*He pauses slightly.*] So at this intersection he veers. An oncoming truck and he veers into its path, so. Leaving no choice but an accident. Terrible accident to erase his life. [*There is a long pause. He takes hold of the steering wheel.*] Can ya get this off when you finish, Bobo Moses? I want it.

BOBO: The fockin' steerin' wheel, eh?

GOODY ABOO: Whole thing. This steering wheel and everything connected on it.

BOBO: What ya do that for? It's a fockin' wreck. Look at it, man. Whole back end. Whole frame's twisted, so. Can't fix it.

GOODY ABOO: I know. But it's the first Chrysler car they ever make in Africa. It is a symbol.

BOBO: It's a piece of the shit, Goody Aboo. What you say it is doesn't make it so.

GOODY ABOO: It's what you sold us for. It is all we have left of the village. I like it.

BOBO: Ain't nothing to like. S'only good for scraps. S'only good for piratin' parts, so. And I ain't giving ya back the engine. It's mine.

GOODY ABOO: Don't want the engine, so.

BOBO: Then it really ain't gonna get ya nowhere.

GOODY ABOO: Got nowhere *to* go. Just told you. So, seems like this is the thing gonna get me there best. [*He sits up as if preparing to drive, pretending to start up the car.*] I'm going to put the pot of my soil from the village. I'm going to put it here on the seat next to me and we will sit together and I will pretend to be moving forward. [*He lights a new* *marijuana cigarette, inhales deeply, and begins to imagine he is moving, enacting the journey as he speaks, lost in the vision and in his perform-ance.*] I will smoke on my *dundun* stick and I will put my hand into the soil in my pot and I will close my eyes and I will sing and I will pre-tend that there is a breeze that is moving over my face and over the lit-tle bit of village soil left in this pot, and I will feel this breeze as Africa is moving forward. I will feel it and know. That we are not wrecked and left for salvaging. That we are not. [*He begins to sing.*] "*Osee Asibe* throws away, throws away to the remotest corner. *Osee Asibe*, child of the Ancient God, dress up as new and let us go. Dress up as if we are new and let us go. Dress us up as new and let us go." [**BOBO** *moves to the car, sliding in alongside* **GOODY ABOO** *and collecting his tools.*]

BOBO: Ought'a crush this thing when I'm done with it. Take it t'a the smelter for melting to pop cans.

GOODY ABOO: Fock you will, eh.

BOBO: Who's gonna stop me? You? Come on now. Got to get out for *Bra Gig* coming.

GOODY ABOO: You're a pirate, Moses Bobo. You're a pirate. Get out. [*He begins pushing* **BOBO** *out of the car.*]

BOBO: What you doing, man? Take it easy. [**BOBO** *resists, and* **GOODY ABOO** *begins pushing harder, beating on him now, pummeling with his fists.*]

GOODY ABOO: No more room for pirates. Get out'a my village, so. Get away from my treasure. Stop piratin' pieces off it. No more.

BOBO: Don't you fockin' take a hand t'a me!

GOODY ABOO: This isn't soda pop cans. Can't make *Baas Piet*'s dream into pop cans.

BOBO: Stop it, man. *Bra Gig* gonna hearin'. [**GOODY ABOO** *begins shouting loudly, thrashing. The beginning of an epileptic seizure comes on him, his hands still flailing and digging at* **BOBO.**]

GOODY ABOO: No more pirates! *Baas Piet! Baas Piet!* No more pirates taking our treasure away!

BOBO: Fock's the matter with you, eh so? [**BOBO** *pushes* **GOODY ABOO** *to the ground and away, where he lays convulsing, shaking and twitching maniacally.*]

GOODY ABOO: They take the ground and they'll take the wheel, *Baas Piet!* Even take that away from us!

BOBO: Stop it. Stop. Look at yourself, eh. Look at what you're doing t'a yourself.

GOODY ABOO: We will be steering! They got the engine, but I'm keeping watch on the wheel! Getting through that intersection! [**GOODY ABOO**'s *seizure gets worse. His words become harder to comprehend, gurgled and spit.*]

BOBO: You're gonna bite off your fockin' tongue, Goody Aboo!

GOODY ABOO: Noo moore Pirrhhaattes!

BOBO: You're having seizures! Ya made yourself get a fockin' seizure, so!

GOODY ABOO: Ttaakkinguh thuh wheeell . . . *Baaas Piet* . . . tthhsst-teeerr!! [**BOBO** *runs to the car and hurriedly tears the steering wheel from the dashboard, then running back to* **GOODY ABOO.**]

BOBO: Fine here. Here. The fockin' wheel. Ya want it, I got it for ya. Bite on it, so. Bite. [*He pries open* **GOODY ABOO**'s *teeth and puts the steering wheel in his mouth.* **GOODY ABOO** *grabs onto it with his two hands, as if steering a moving car.*]

GOODY ABOO: Tthhsstteeerr . . . tthhsstteeerr . . . ! [*The convulsions quiet a little.* **GOODY ABOO** *calms, almost passing out, but maintaining a firm grip on the wheel. There is a pause.* **BOBO** *rises, standing back from him and staring.*]

BOBO: Okay. Okay, eh so.

GOODY ABOO: [*Quietly.*] Tthhsstteeerr . . . tthhsstteeerr . . .

BOBO: Yeah. Fockin' steer. Steer wherever ya want, Salvage *Baas.* Got treasure you're holding in your hands. Ya salvaged it. Fockin' treasure chest wherever ya look. [*There is a long pause,* **GOODY ABOO**'s *subsiding seizure and his labored breathing the only sound.* **BOBO** *stands helplessly amidst his pirated parts. A tableau of the two men before the shell of the car. Blackout.*]

DISSATISFACTION #4

by Jeff Tabnick

CHARACTERS:

Vic: Male, late 20s

Tiny: Female, late 20s

SETTING:

Kitchen.

TIME:

Morning.

NOTE: When the dialogue is [between brackets] it is not spoken; it is just an indication of what the character would say if he/she were to continue speaking.

JEFF TABNICK'S plays have been presented by LaMaMa ETC, Ensemble Studio Theatre, The Riant Theatre Company, and The Atlantic Theater Company Acting School. He is a co-founder of Propinquity Productions LLC, which has produced several of his one-act and full-length plays-including *Barrymore's Body* at the NYC Fringe Festival 2004. He is currently co-writing a screenplay, *Time Machine Girlfriends.*

Dissatisfaction #4 was first directed by Meghan McCarthy and presented at Developing Artists' Rebel Verses Festival. It was then produced by Third Man Productions as part of their Bar Hoppers Series.

Early morning. Kitchen. VIC, *in a cheap black suit and blue tinted glasses—a rock 'n' roll star wanna-be—drinks his coffee and reads the paper.* VIC *frequently mumbles.* TINY *enters in a conservative dress or blouse and skirt. She's still waking up.* TINY *is soft-spoken and her sentences frequently trail off. Throughout, they are making and eating breakfast. They drink coffee, make toast, do the dishes, cleanup—whatever the set will allow for. If the set only allows for them to sit at a table and eat muffins and drink coffee that* VIC *previously bought at the deli across the street and brought home in a paper bag for breakfast, that's fine too.*

VIC: Mornin'.

TINY: Hi. [VIC *gives* TINY *a peck on the lips,* TINY *lingers for a moment then turns her attention to breakfast.*]

VIC: So, how about last night? [*Beat.*]

TINY: . . . I thought you were gonna wear a shirt and jeans . . .

VIC: You're welcome.

TINY: I can't believe you don't have a suit.

VIC: What is this on my body?

TINY: Before, I mean as something to . . . have.

VIC: I haven't been to a wedding [since—] [*Looking in the sink . . .*]
Why am I the only one who does the dishes in this relationship? [*Beat.*]

TINY: You get sick of them quicker than I do?

VIC: Hey.

TINY: Hey?

VIC: So.

TINY: So?

VIC: You fell asleep right afterwards . . .

TINY: [*Underneath.*] I was so tired afterwards.

VIC: [*Continuous.*] . . . we didn't get to *talk* about it.

TINY: So unbelievably unexpectedly tired.

VIC: [*Mumbled.*] I mean it was over, I . . . and you—and I looked down and you—asleep. [TINY *nods, smiles politely, and looks away.*] Well and before, you drank a lot at the bar before.

TINY: I wasn't drunk when we . . .

VIC: Cool. That's cool. I thought maybe that was why.

TINY: [*Offended.*] Because I was—

VIC: [*Over.*] I don't *know* why.

TINY: [*Over.*] That's not, that's—I wasn't.

VIC: [*Very concerned.*] That's the only thing. *Why you wanted to.* Why last night. That's all. *I just don't know.*

TINY: Well. Um . . . [*Long beat until* VIC *gives up on an answer.*]

VIC: [*Over.*] I always thought I would be too squeamish to—personally

TINY: [*Over, timidly.*] Did you see those two gay men at the bar?

VIC: Guys would be like, would you, and I would be like I don't know, would you? *I* don't think so.

TINY: [*Even more timidly.*] You know what it was like?

VIC: *I didn't know why I would do it*—What was it like?

TINY: No, it's too—never . . . [mind.]

VIC: What?

TINY: It's really too early in the [morning] for this [conversation] . . .

VIC: What was it like?

TINY: Cindy will be here in 10 [minutes].

VIC: What what what what

TINY: She'll honk when she [gets here].

VIC: [*Continuous.*] what what what what what

TINY: [*Continuous.*] We can't keep her [waiting].

VIC: what what was it like?

TINY: It reminded me of when I lost my [virginity]—That's what it reminded me of.

VIC: [*Overlapping at "That's."*] *Really?* Cool.

TINY: [*Over.*] Jeez.

VIC: [*Over.*] Holy shit.

TINY: I buy a lot of things around here!

VIC: Holy shit.

TINY: That's why maybe you do the dishes, because I buy more around here than you do! That's why maybe.

VIC: You do?

TINY: Well, the *shampoo* that's all I'm [saying]—Hey and what we did. Last night. It's not an every time [thing].

VIC: [*Underneath.*] I know.

TINY: [*Continuous.*] And my Biore, I know you use my face cleanser. Not that I mind but.

VIC: [*Overlapping after "cleanser."*] I know that, it's not an every time —I

TINY: It's expensive, and maybe you don't realize. That's all. You didn't know *why you would* do it? I don't [understand].

VIC: It's not that I wouldn't—you never—and I know you know I use your Biore by the way—that's like two different things, two different categories. Buying and cleaning. Two different categories—

TINY: So, um, last night—

VIC: [*Eagerly.*] Last night, yes—

TINY: —these two gay men were in the bar last night, did you see— [*Then, over:*] After your gig.

VIC: [*Over.*] So what?

TINY: So, listen, I'm trying to—

VIC: [*Continuous.*] This isn't what I want to talk about.

TINY: It was upsetting. Actually.

VIC: *It* was?

TINY: These two gay men that walked into the bar—

VIC: *Why* was that—?

TINY: These two gay men walked into the bar—

VIC: Stop me if you've heard this one before.

TINY: This isn't a joke—

VIC: I'll be the judge of that.

TINY: Vic.

VIC: What?

TINY: About an hour after your set was over.

VIC: We played good last night, didn't we? The crowd was into it. People were dancing. Some people even knew the words.

TINY: *You* were good.

VIC: No, they're a good—

TINY: It's just that maybe. Your drummer can't keep a.

VIC: He's getting better!

TINY: He's getting [better]? [*Then, over:*] How long have you guys been playing?

VIC: [*Over, angry.*] I mean we're not good like other bands are good, so what?

TINY: [*Backing off.*] You seem to like tending bar, and if that pays your half of the bills then I don't see why you shouldn't—It's not like I'm so happy at my [job]—I'm not saying you should become a [investment banker]—We can't keep Cindy waiting when she honks, she's paranoid that she'll be shot in *this* neighborhood.

VIC: I've never even seen any gay people in that bar.

TINY: You were too busy.

VIC: Performing.

TINY: . . . flirting . . .

VIC: I wasn't flirting with her.

TINY: You know who I'm . . .

VIC: I hadn't seen her in a.

TINY: Ol' sloppy breasts.

VIC: She hasn't come to one of my gigs in a—

TINY: You ever do *that* with ol' sloppy breasts?

VIC: That was years ago. [*Then, over:*] Not *that*. Not what we—
I mean *when* we—

TINY: [*Over.*] Really?

VIC: I mean when we were—Is that why we did that last night?

TINY: No!

VIC: Because I was talking to ol' sloppy breasts?

TINY: I said no.

VIC: I didn't think anyone I ever dated would do it.

TINY: You dated a lot. Do you—

VIC: Yeah . . .

TINY: You don't think I'm.

VIC: What?

TINY: Trashy?

VIC: No. I mean yeah—I dated a lot. I didn't think I'd like it.

TINY: Did you like it?

VIC: It didn't hurt you?

TINY: Did you like it?

VIC: It didn't hurt you?

TINY: Did you like it?

VIC: Yeah.

TINY: It didn't hurt me.

VIC: But.

TINY: Only me though, right?

VIC: But *why* is my question. [*Answering her previous question.*] But yeah. Yes.

TINY: [*Over.*] So you didn't see the gay men?

VIC: [*Over.*] You know it's not like you have your period.

TINY: You didn't see what happened?

VIC: Was it something you'd been thinking about . . . doing?

TINY: Well—I. I'm trying to [explain]. You know, I also buy the paper towels, the toilet paper, the toothpaste, the soap, the cleaning supplies, the—Vic, I buy a lot! By the way. That just. Occurred to me. That's all. I'm sorry.

VIC: [*Over.*] We've lived together for three years, *Tiny*—so—so.

TINY: [*Over.*] So, so, and all you do is moan and—when you do the.

VIC: Whatever.

TINY: *Dishes.*

VIC: Two different categories.

TINY: You held me all night *so tight* last night.

VIC: Well the whole experience was . . .

TINY: I didn't think it would be tender.

VIC: I didn't want you to think it was . . .

TINY: We've never . . . cuddled all night before.

VIC: [*Underneath.*] I wanted you to know.

TINY: [*Continuous.*] No the only night we ever cuddled all night before . . .

VIC: . . . was after that bad thing happened.

TINY: Right.

VIC: Right. Well again I wanted you to know. [**TINY** *smiles.*]

TINY: Good. *Exactly.* [*Long beat; then, tenderly:*] It's a very nice [suit], blue would've looked nice on you too.

VIC: I was thinking about buying a zoot suit.

TINY: Black is fine.

VIC: I'll be prepared when someone dies.

TINY: Morbid.

VIC: As long as I'm not the first to go, the black suit was a good investment. If I am the first to go, though, I really should have bought the zoot suit. It's like a suit but with more zoo and less sue. Bury me in a zoot suit. Marriage is the first step to death.

TINY: Birth is the first step to death.

VIC: That's trite.

TINY: It's true.

VIC: It's boring. Why do people get married?

TINY: Why do they move in together?

VIC: [*Seriously.*] Financial reasons.

TINY: [*Very hurt.*] Oh.

VIC: And *a lot* of reasons. It's not like *we* couldn't get out of this.

TINY: Going to this wedding?

VIC: Living in this apartment. [*Beat.*]

TINY: [*On the verge of tears.*] Is that a. [**VIC** *opens his mouth to continue but* **TINY** *looks so upset that he can't.*]

VIC: [*Defeated.*] Or going to this wedding.

TINY: [*As if that is what he was talking about all along.*] You know, if you don't want to go, you can just say that and I will go to this—

VIC: I'm wearing the fucking suit!

TINY: [*Mournful.*] Wedding.

VIC: It's on my fucking body! [*Beat.*]

TINY: Alone. [*Beat. Then, bravely:*] People our age [get married].

VIC: [*Quick, defensive.*] People our age what?

TINY: Go to weddings!

VIC: That's *why* last night—right?!—why we did that in bed—because we're going to some *bitch's* wedding today—

TINY: That's not nice to call her a—

VIC: [*Overlapping after "nice."*] —I didn't mean "bitch" in a bad way—

TINY: And it's *not*—

VIC: [*Vehemently.*] —right?!—and you knew I'd freak out so you were trying to keep me [interested in you]—right!?

TINY: Keep you what?

VIC: You know!

TINY: Not unless you say it!

VIC: Well, then why?

TINY: Two gay men came into the bar . . .

VIC: Jesus fucking Christ!

TINY: [*Continuous.*] . . . and they were *very* drunk. [*Then, over.*] I'm going to finish this—

VIC: [*Over.*] This—*avoidance!*

TINY: —*this*—

VIC: Fine!

TINY: —*story!*

VIC: Fine!

TINY: They started arguing—

VIC: [*Wearily feigning interest.*] About what?

TINY: —raising their, *I don't know*, they get drunker *that's not the point* and now they are yelling, calling each other *bad* names, pushing, *punching* each other . . .

VIC: With fists?

TINY: [*Continuous.*] The face, like head— [TINY *mimes head butting.*]

VIC: No shit. [*As* TINY *continues and gets worked up, words come hard to her, but she battles on anyway.*]

TINY: Bleeding, both of them, still punching, and three huge Harley Davidson . . . *bald* guys with these . . . *beards* have to pull them apart and . . . *pin* them down. The Harley Davidson guys back away and the two men lie on the ground, they're *breathing* heavy, their chests are *heaving* up and down. Then they get up. Then I see them through the window and they're standing on the sidewalk holding each other *so tight.* And I thought look how lucky gay couples are.

VIC: [*Not understanding at all, laughing.*] What?

TINY: [*Unable to conceal the raw anger in her voice.*] They can punch each other. [VIC *laughs, but then, just for a moment he allows himself to understand.*]

VIC: Right.

TINY: And then *we* went home. And [we went to bed].

VIC: I understand why you wanted to tell it so badly.

TINY: You do?

VIC: [*As if it's all been a joke . . .*] It is very funny. Usually I'm the funny one, but that is very funny. [*Car honks.*]

TINY: I guess it is . . .

VIC: Oh on our way back home try to remember we need to buy dental floss.

TINY: Make sure you wash that pan you left in the [stove]. It's starting to [smell]. [*They exit. Blackout.*]

FOUL TERRITORY

by Craig Wright

CHARACTERS:

Owen: Male, 30s–40s

Ruth: Female, 30s–40s

Announcer

CRAIG WRIGHT'S plays include *The Pavilion* (City Theatre, Actors Theatre of Louisville, the Globe Theatres), *Main Street* (Great American History Theatre), *Orange Flower Water* (CATF, the Jungle, Steppenwolf), *Recent Tragic Events* (Woolly Mammoth, Playwrights Horizons), *Molly's Delicious* (Arden Theatre), and *Melissa Arctic* (Folger Theatre). He is currently working on commissions from CATF, Woolly Mammoth, and Actors Theatre of Louisville, and has just completed his second season writing for *Six Feet Under*. His plays are published by Dramatists Play Service, Playscripts Inc., Dramatic Publishing, and Smith and Kraus. He has received several awards for his writing, including fellowships from the McKnight Foundation and the National Endowment for the Arts. He holds an M.Div. degree from United Theological Seminary and lives in Los Angeles with his wife, Lorraine LeBlanc, and their son, Louis.

The scene is a row of far left-field seats at Yankee Stadium. OWEN *is* seated next to RUTH. *Throughout the scene we can hear a baseball game in progress; the distant drone of the* ANNOUNCER *giving the play-by-play; the general crowd roar; and the periodic crack of the bat hitting the ball.* OWEN *and* RUTH *are both eating popcorn or peanuts. We hear the crack of the bat hitting the ball.* RUTH *jumps out of her seat.*

RUTH: Yeah, Bernie! Way to go! Way to bloop that ball in there!!! [*She settles back into her seat.*] I think they're gonna do it this year, Owen. I can feel it. They're going all the way. Three months from now, mark my words, it's the World Series, and we'll be sitting here winnin' it . . . [*She eats a mouthful of popcorn, then finishes her thought with her mouth full.*]

ANNOUNCER: NOW BATTING . . . NUMBER TWO . . . DEREK JETER.

RUTH: Mark my words. [*Another big mouthful—and she turns to* OWEN—] Don'tcha think? [*—to catch him eyeing her with pity.*]

RUTH: What? What are you looking at? What?

OWEN: [*After a beat, pityingly.*] You're so brave.

RUTH: Gimme a break.

OWEN: No, I mean it, Ruth, you are—

RUTH: Because I think the *Yankees* have a chance? It doesn't take a genius—

OWEN: No, to be out here like this, like you are.

RUTH: At the game?

OWEN: At the game, at the whole thing! [*We hear the crack of the bat hitting the ball.*] To be getting back on your feet the way you're getting—after what Tom did to you—you're so sweet and brave— [*He eats a single piece of popcorn, gazing at her. She tracks the approaching ball with her eyes.*] —so sweet and brave

RUTH: Stop it.

OWEN: No, I mean it, you're, like, straight outta Laura Ingalls Wilder, I'm so proud of you, to bounce back like this. After Monty left me— [*A ball sails in and cracks* OWEN *loudly on the head*—] OW!

RUTH: Oh God! Oh God, Owen, are you alright? Oh God!

OWEN: [*Holding his head.*] I'm fine, I'm fine—

RUTH: Didn't you see that coming?

OWEN: Yeah, I, I kinda did . . .

RUTH: It was coming right at you—

OWEN: I know—

RUTH: Oh my God . . . do you need anything? Ice, or—

OWEN: No—

RUTH: Should we take you to First Aid or something?

OWEN: No, I'm fine! I'm good. Really. Just watch your game, honey. Enjoy yourself. It's your night. It's your night.

RUTH: You're sure?

OWEN: Yes—

RUTH: Because we can go, really—

OWEN: [*Still rocking, in terrible pain.*] No, I'm shakin' it off. I'm a trooper. I'm fine.

RUTH: [*Double-checking.*] You're absolutely sure?

OWEN: Yes.

RUTH: [*Doubtfully.*] OK. OK. You're sure you're alright?

OWEN: Yep. Par for the course. I'm fine.

RUTH: OK. OK. [*She settles back into watching the game. A moment passes. Something catches her eye.*] Did you see that?

OWEN: No, what?

RUTH: He balked. [*To the field.*] Stay on the rubber! [*After a long beat.*] Look, he did it again— [*She stands and screams at the field.*] *Stay on the rubber! This isn't Cuba, pal!* [*To* OWEN.] Do you see what I'm talkin' about?

OWEN: [*Still rubbing his head.*] No, I—I missed it—

RUTH: He balks, like, every third pitch, this guy, and no one calls it! No one ever calls it! [*Amazed.*] Jesus. [*She sits back down, eats some popcorn.*] What's the point of having a rule if no one's gonna call it?

OWEN: Have you heard from him? At all?

RUTH: I don't want to talk about it—

OWEN: Wouldja take him back?

RUTH: No! [*We hear the crack of the bat hitting the ball.*] You don't get it, Owen, Tom Scintilla leaving me is the *best thing* that ever could have happened—to me or the kids—

OWEN: But you miss him—

RUTH: I don't—

OWEN: Oh, come on, you miss him and you want him back, just admit it. When Monty left me— [*The ball sails in and hits him hard in the face.*] OW!!

RUTH: [*Angry and concerned.*] Owen, move!! [*Blood sprays from his nose. He clutches it in agony.*]

OWEN: When?

RUTH: *When you see the ball coming!* God! Are you alright? You're bleeding!

OWEN: I am?

RUTH: Is anything broken?

OWEN: No, it just . . . it just kinda . . . *hurts* . . . [*She pulls a napkin from her popcorn container and anxiously dabs his nose, trying to soak up some of the blood.*] Ow, ow, ow . . .

RUTH: [*After a beat, with one eye on the game.*] So you saw that coming?

OWEN: Of course!

RUTH: So why didn't you *move?*

OWEN: What would be the point?

RUTH: What the hell does that mean? Jesus— [*She suddenly stands up and screams at the field.*] *Would someone please nail this guy's feet to the motherfuckin' rubber or make the call??* Jesus Christ! [**RUTH** *sits back down, annoyed with the game.*] I mean, this guy's not gonna cost us the game, but *shit!* [*A moment passes as she eats some popcorn and looks at* **OWEN.**] So what do you mean, "what would be the point?"

OWEN: It doesn't matter—

RUTH: Sure it does—

OWEN: No, you're enjoying the game—

RUTH: No, tell me! I've been going to baseball games for 35 years, Owen, I never caught a foul ball once and I just saw you get hit twice in one game!

OWEN: That's life—

RUTH: No, it's not life, it's fuckin' weird! [*Then, responding approvingly to the field.*] Ball four! There! Thank you! Thank you! [*To* OWEN.] Do you realize, now, with Bernie and Derek on base, if A-Rod hits a home run, it's over, right?

OWEN: Yeah—

RUTH: This is a good game—All right! They're changing pitchers! Take a hike, you bum!

OWEN: When I got hit in the face with a baseball the *first* time—

RUTH: [*Caught off-guard.*] How many times have you been hit?

OWEN: I don't know, a lot.

RUTH: You never told me this—

OWEN: It never came up—we never went to a game—

RUTH: I guess you're right—

OWEN: —the first time I was eleven years old, trying to catch a pop fly in the street—

RUTH: You played baseball?

OWEN: I know, it's unlikely—

RUTH: It's mega-unlikely—

OWEN: Well, I did, and this kid hit a pop fly and I must have mis-judged or something, the important part is BANG, I got hit right between the eyes.

RUTH: Ouch.

OWEN: Yeah. There was blood everywhere, my eyes were swollen shut—

RUTH: Go—

OWEN: Yeah, and I got totally got spooked. [*He blows his nose and the napkin fills with blood.*]

RUTH: Are you sure you're alright?

OWEN: Yeah, I just feel a little . . . a little faint, anyway, a couple days later, I was at a baseball game for my school—not even playing, I was just doing stats, because my vision was still a little screwed up, and Jonny Blank hit a high foul and I freaked out. Everyone else was just sitting there, and I'm screaming, running around like a bee is chasing me and I'm ALREADY crying and I finally find the spot where I'm safe and I crouch down and cover my ears, but then I hear somebody catch it, so I look up and BANG, it hits me in the face!

RUTH: Oh my God!

OWEN: I know!

RUTH: What are the chances?

OWEN: Very high, obviously—

RUTH: [*Affirmatively.*] I guess—

OWEN: Anyway, I spent the next week in the hospital.

RUTH: The hospital?

OWEN: Kind of a . . . mental hospital—

RUTH: Oh—

OWEN: —and when I got out, my father, my beloved father whom I must have generated in my previous life in some evil DUNGEON, fabricated him from trash like some Golem, you know, to torture me later in case I forgot what was true about GOD, my beloved father decided to take me to a baseball game. He told me I had to get back on the horse. I cried the whole way in the car, "Don't take me. Turn around. I want to go home." He didn't care. We got to the game and lo and behold—

RUTH: You got hit—

OWEN: No. Nothing happened. [*After a beat.*] For eight innings.

RUTH: Oh no—

OWEN: And then Lou Piniella hit a high foul into the stands, and my father said "Just sit still," and I did—for two seconds—and then I RAN up the stairs into an empty row that looked safe and BANG, it caught me right in the ear!

RUTH: No!

OWEN: Yes! I still can't hear anything in this ear! I point this ear at something, I hear the ocean. MAYBE.

RUTH: That's amazing.

ANNOUNCER: NOW BATTING . . . NUMBER THIRTEEN . . . ALEX RODRIGUEZ.

OWEN: We can't run, Ruth, that's my point. Whether it's baseballs or heartbreak, whether it's your Tom or my Monty, there's no escaping it. Life is going to destroy us. It's going to. Letting it happen is the only freedom we have.

RUTH: But Owen, that's absurd—

OWEN: It's the truth!

RUTH: But Owen, I'm happier now than I've been in ten years! The house is clean, all of Tom's stupid model train stuff is outta there; the kids are doing better in school; Carla Kendall is setting me up next week with a really nice guy—

OWEN: [*Doubtful.*] Oh, right—

RUTH: He sounds really sweet, he's a personal trainer—

OWEN: Sure he is—

RUTH: I think things are really looking up!

OWEN: And I think you're kidding yourself! I think you're seriously kidding yourself. [*We hear a loud crack of the bat hitting the ball. Then, fatalistically:*] See, here it comes again— [RUTH *stands up.*]

RUTH: Catch it!

OWEN: No, there's no point!

RUTH: Owen, stand up, put out your hands and catch it! [*She pulls him up.*]

OWEN: But if I reach here, the ball goes there, Ruth, wherever I reach is where it won't be!

RUTH: That can't be true!

OWEN: [*Indicating his bloody nose.*] Look at me, Ruth, if anything's true, it's true, I know my own life—

RUTH: Put out your hands! [*She puts out his hands.*] Now keep your eyes open, keep your eye on the ball, and catch it!

OWEN: OK, I'll try!

RUTH: Here it comes . . . here it comes . . . here it comes . . . [*Their eyes track the incoming ball. OWEN's ready to catch it. Boom, it hits OWEN in the face with a loud smack. He falls over, clutching his face in quiet agony. RUTH doesn't react in horror this time. She just looks down at him. Then, after a long beat:*] But see, aren't you glad you made the effort?

OWEN: [*From down on the ground, curled up in pain, after a beat.*] Yeah, I'm glad.

RUTH: You'll get the next one. Just tell yourself, "I'll get the next one."

OWEN: "I'll get the next one."

RUTH: You can't lose hope, Owen. That's what I tell the kids. We can't lose hope. It's all we've got. [*She sits down, eats some popcorn, watches the field with interest.*] I really think we have a shot this year. I think we're really gonna go all the way. [*Loud crack of the bat hitting the ball. End.*]

SAD SONG

A ten-minute play
by Anna Ziegler

CHARACTERS:

Rachel: Female, 18–22

Charlie: Male, 18–22

Jordan: Male, 18–22

SETTING:

A bedroom, dimly lit.

ANNA ZIEGLER graduated from Yale College in 2001 and the
University of East Anglia's Master's in Creative Writing (Poetry)
program in 2002. Her plays have been read or produced in the NYU
Festival of New Works; at The Lark Theatre, The Kennedy Center,
The Tank Theater, and Theatre Limina; and by the Fireraisers at the
Hampstead Theatre (London) and Company B at the Belvoir St.
Theatre (Sydney, Australia). She's been published in *Ten-Minute Plays
for 2 Actors: The Best of 2002/2003* (Smith and Kraus, Inc.), and her
poetry has appeared in *Best American Poetry 2003*, *The Threepenny
Review*, *The Michigan Quarterly Review*, *The Mississippi Review*, *Arts
and Letters*, *Mid-American Review*, *The Saint Ann's Review*, and many
other journals. In 2004 she graduated from the MFA program in
Dramatic Writing at NYU's Tisch School of the Arts, and is currently
teaching creative writing at George Washington University.

SONG

When I am dead, my dearest,
Sing no sad songs for me;
Plant thou no roses at my head,
Nor shady cypress tree:
Be the green grass above me
With showers and dewdrops wet;
And if thou wilt, remember,
And if thou wilt, forget.

I shall not see the shadows,
I shall not feel the rain;
I shall not hear the nightingale
Sing on, as if in pain:
And dreaming through the twilight
That doth not rise nor set,
Haply I may remember,
And haply may forget.

—C. ROSSETTI

In a bedroom. Outside, a loud party. **RACHEL** *and* **JORDAN** *sit side by side on the bed, at an awkward distance. They've both been drinking, to varying degrees.* **RACHEL** *holds a drink.* Silence. They look at each other.

RACHEL: Um, I'm not sure we should do this.

JORDAN: Do what? We're sitting here—

RACHEL: What if they hear us? Charlie'll go crazy. You know how he gets. Remember when Sarah—

JORDAN: Sure, in the laundry room. Who could forget.

RACHEL: I mean, he still hates her for that.

JORDAN: Come on . . . the music's loud.

RACHEL: I know but—

JORDAN: What?

RACHEL: I don't know. [*He leans over and kisses her neck.*]

JORDAN: Charlie's drunk anyway. He's sloshed. He's gone.

RACHEL: [*Taking a sip.*] *I'm* a little drunk.

JORDAN: You're always a little drunk. That's what I like about you. You're an adorable little drunk, baby.

RACHEL: I feel bad for him.

JORDAN: He's fine . . . that was months ago. He's fine. He's a rebounder. He's back in the game of life. He's totally grabbing it by the horns . . . I mean, have you watched him at all tonight? He's loose.

RACHEL: I don't know; when *my* mother— [JORDAN *groans.* RACHEL *looks at him.*]

JORDAN: You don't want to talk about that now, do you?

RACHEL: I had such awful dreams. I mean, I still have them some-times, but I had them every night then . . . [*Beat.*] Once, she told me to open a box in the attic, and when I woke up, I realized we didn't have an attic . . . I felt all of a sudden like there were no mysteries in the world, after all. No revelations. I hadn't realized that I wanted there to be mysteries and then there weren't any. [JORDAN*'s waited long enough. Now he smiles drunkenly and takes hold of* RACHEL, *starts kiss-*

ing her aggressively. The music gets louder. **JORDAN** *takes a breath.*]

JORDAN: [*In his own world.*] The music is so fucking loud, Rachel. No one even knows we're in here. [*He pulls her shirt off. Someone outside shouts a request and the song changes to "These Are the Days."* **RACHEL** *stands and sways.*]

RACHEL: Oh, I love this song.

JORDAN: You look hot when you dance like that.

RACHEL: I love it and it makes me sad. Isn't that a strange combination?

JORDAN: Move your hips some more.

RACHEL: It makes me forget where I am. I feel like I'm in high school again standing under the bridge at 1 AM drinking awful beer slowly under this, like, incredibly clear sky full of stars that have always been there and will always be there, and I have some vague sense that I should try to remember who I am right now because I won't be like this for long.

JORDAN: [*He stands and puts his arms around her.*] You're still you. [*She breaks away and walks to the door.*]

RACHEL: [*Putting her ear to the door.*] I love this song. It makes me so fucking sad. [*The door opens into* **RACHEL**, *thrusting her backwards.* **CHARLIE** *enters.*]

CHARLIE: Oh God—are you okay? I didn't mean to—I didn't know anyone was—

RACHEL: I'm fine. [**CHARLIE** *looks from* **RACHEL** *to* **JORDAN**. *He looks back at* **RACHEL**. *Her shirt's off. She covers her chest with her hands.*]

CHARLIE: [*REALLY awkward and slow, as though he has to search for every word.*] Sorry, I was just coming in to get that, uh, book, from the table, by the bed.

JORDAN: [*Throwing it to him.*] Here.

CHARLIE: I just wanted to show someone this, um, book. So, anyway, I'm leaving now. [*He starts to leave.*]

RACHEL: You don't have to go. [**RACHEL** *drops her hands from her chest.*]

JORDAN: That's okay. We'll be out in a sec, kay, Charlie? 5 You go show off that book.

RACHEL: Stay.

CHARLIE: Stay?

JORDAN: Stay?

RACHEL: What's this book?

CHARLIE: [*He can't stop staring at her chest;* **JORDAN** *notices.*] Oh no . . . it's nothing. It's stupid.

JORDAN: [*Throwing* **RACHEL** *her shirt, annoyed, then:*] Here.

CHARLIE: You know, Julie's gonna take out the guitar soon. That should be good. She's gonna play, like, requests.

RACHEL: What's the book about?

CHARLIE: The book? Well, it's about . . . I wasn't really going to show it to everyone. Just to Julie. She wanted to see it. It's about . . . well, about mourning, really.

JORDAN: Me, I'd prefer a book about night. More shit happens at night. I can barely wake up in the morning.

CHARLIE: No, it's about the grieving process, I guess. About the stages of grieving . . . funny stuff, eh?

RACHEL: It's not funny.

CHARLIE: No, but—

RACHEL: Charlie, are you with Julie?

CHARLIE: Am I with Julie?

RACHEL: I always see you together. On campus. In the library.

CHARLIE: Well, we have a lot of classes together.

JORDAN: [*Matter-of-factly.*] But you are fucking her, right?

CHARLIE: No.

JORDAN: That's a totally missed opportunity. She wants you, man.

CHARLIE: No, I don't think so. Not that I—well I never . . . can tell, with anyone . . . I mean once this girl, well you wouldn't know her, but she had to ask me to kiss her— [**JORDAN** *groans in shock.*] . . . Yeah, then finally I knew . . .

RACHEL: Do you like her?

JORDAN: She's hot. He's into her.

CHARLIE: I'm not.

RACHEL: [*After a beat, to* **CHARLIE.**] We're sorry for coming in here. I know you don't like people in your room.

CHARLIE: It's fine.

RACHEL: We weren't doing anything, just so you know.

JORDAN: Well maybe we were about to . . .

RACHEL: We weren't.

CHARLIE: You know, I think I hear the guitar. I'm gonna go out there —I promised Julie I'd be there to hear her songs. She wrote a few new ones. She might record something this fall. She might make an album. Who knows.

RACHEL: [*To* **CHARLIE.**] I was thinking about you.

CHARLIE: What?

JORDAN: She's worried you're still, like, distraught. I tried to tell her you've totally bucked up. That you're totally in the game, but she won't listen. She's always worrying. You get some drink in her and she just worries. What's the point of drinking?

RACHEL: I've been thinking about you all night.

CHARLIE: You have?

RACHEL: I wondered if you have dreams . . .

CHARLIE: Yeah . . . I have all sorts of dreams . . .

JORDAN: OK. If this is going to be some kind of weird "my mom died" club, I'm just gonna go. [*No one says anything;* **JORDAN** *doesn't move.*] Though, if you must know, I don't like my mom all that much. She totally annoys the hell out of me when she calls to see if I've been sleeping enough. I mean, is that really the most important thing? What about, like, eating? And she always bugs me when I'm completely hung-over, my head banging like a—

RACHEL: [*Interrupting.*] Jordan, could you excuse us a few minutes?

CHARLIE: [*Confused.*] Excuse us?

RACHEL: [*To* **JORDAN.**] We'll be out soon. Go get a beer. I want to talk to Charlie.

JORDAN: I'm not going anywhere.

CHARLIE: How bout *I* go— [*He starts to leave again.*]

RACHEL: [*To* CHARLIE, *really fast, as though without thinking.*] I wanted to tell you that I think I love you.

JORDAN: Whoa, whoa there. Wait just a second—

RACHEL: I want to help you.

JORDAN: You have had *way* too much to drink. [*To* CHARLIE.] She must have had some when I wasn't looking. [*He takes her arm.*] Let's go.

RACHEL: I've loved you since the night you kissed me under the bridge in ninth grade. I don't know why I never called you back.

CHARLIE: [*Turning around, finally.*] You're fucking with me.

RACHEL: No.

CHARLIE: You don't even talk to me. If I wasn't friends with Sarah, you wouldn't ever see me.

RACHEL: That's not true.

JORDAN: Hey, what's going on here?

CHARLIE: You didn't call me back because you wished you hadn't kissed me. You told Sarah I was a bad kisser. You told her I was boring. I remember.

RACHEL: I didn't.

JORDAN: You kissed *this* guy?

RACHEL: It was a long time ago.

CHARLIE: Yeah, so why the hell are you bringing it up now?

RACHEL: I can't get you out of my mind.

JORDAN: Hey, don't mind her. She's nuts. She's completely crazy sometimes. Sometimes she tells me she doesn't know how to get through the day . . . I mean, what does that mean?

CHARLIE: [*Quietly.*] Beats me. [**CHARLIE** *stares at* **RACHEL** *for a few moments, shakes his head, and then leaves, closing the door behind him.* **RACHEL** *stares at the door. Beat.* **JORDAN** *comes up behind her and begins to kiss her neck.*]

RACHEL: [*Breaking away from him.*] Don't do that.

JORDAN: Why not, baby.

RACHEL: I don't know.

JORDAN: You're so full of shit sometimes. Why would you tell that guy you love him?

RACHEL: I don't know.

JORDAN: Okay, well, don't do that anymore, all right? It kind of unnerves me . . . It's like that moment in baseball when you think a ball might go all the way and then it dips foul. You think you know something, and then you don't . . . Or like in hockey when the puck is going straight towards the goal and then it gets deflected at the last second by someone on *your own* team. Total waste. That kind of thing.

RACHEL: [*Quietly.*] Okay.

JORDAN: So don't unnerve me.

RACHEL: Okay. [*Lights down. End of play.*]

PERFORMANCE RIGHTS INFORMATION

CAUTION: *Professionals and amateurs are hereby warned that the plays in this anthology are subject to a royalty. They are fully protected under the copyright laws of the United States of America, and of all countries covered by the International Copyright Union (including the Dominion of Canada and the rest of the British Commonwealth), and of all countries covered by the Pan-American Copyright Convention, and all countries with which the United States has reciprocal copyright relations. All rights, including professional, amateur, motion picture, recitation, lecturing, public reading, radio broadcasting, television, video or sound taping, all other forms of mechanical or electronic reproduction, such as information storage and retrieval systems and photo-copyright, and the rights of translation into foreign language are strictly reserved. Particular emphasis is laid upon the question of readings, permission for which must be secured from the author or his/her agent in writing.*

THE SECOND BEAM Copyright © 2004 by Joan Ackermann. All rights reserved. Reprinted by permission of the author. All inquiries regarding performance rights should be addressed to Scott D. Edwards, Harden-Curtis Agency, 850 Seventh Avenue #903, New York, NY, 10019.

A BODY OF WATER Copyright © 2004 by Neena Beber. All rights reserved. Reprinted by permission of the author. All inquiries regarding performance rights should be addressed to Neena Beber, 380 West 12th Street #6F, New York, NY, 10014.

HELP Copyright © 2004 by Neena Beber. All rights reserved. Reprinted by permission of the author. All inquiries regarding performance rights should be addressed to Neena Beber, 380 West 12th Street #6F, New York, NY, 10014.

DEFUSION Copyright © 2004 by Brooke Berman. All rights reserved. Reprinted by permission of the author. All inquiries regarding performance rights should be addressed to Michael Cardonick, c/o Creative Artists Agency, 162 5th Avenue, 6th Floor, New York, NY, 10010.

ALL WE CAN HANDLE Copyright © 2004 by Andrew Dainoff. All rights reserved. Reprinted by permission of the author. All inquiries regarding performance rights should be addressed to Andrew Dainoff, 447 East 14th Street #3D, New York, NY, 10009.

Printed in the United States
126434LV00004B/47/A